creative
BATIK

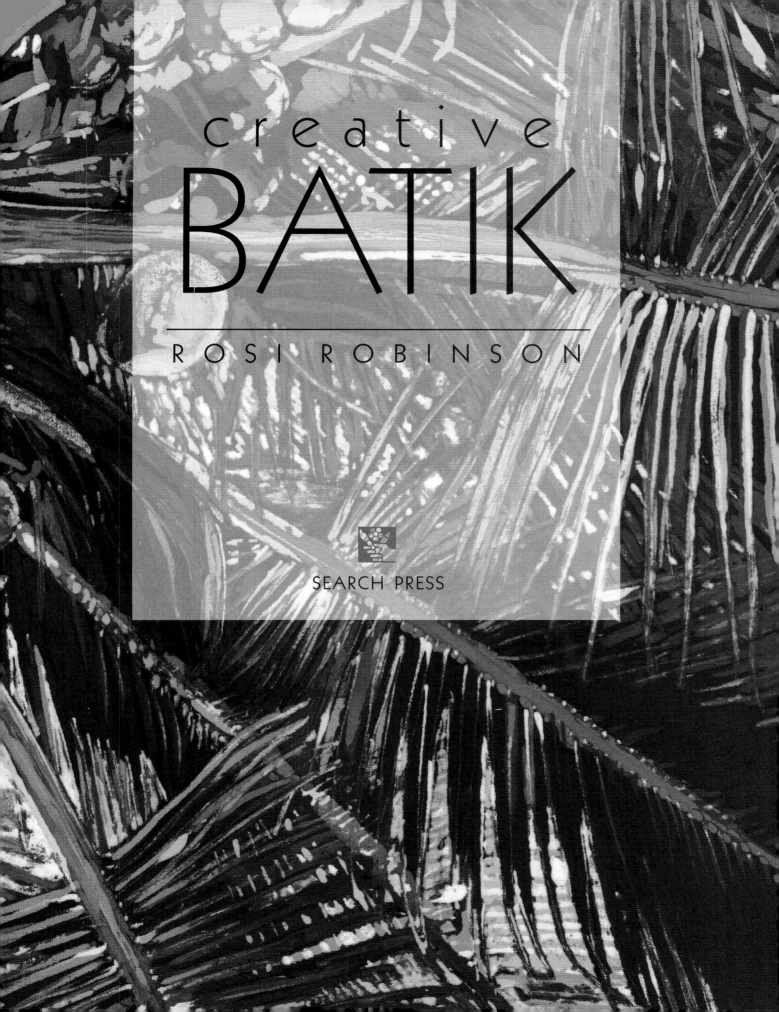

creative
BATIK

ROSI ROBINSON

SEARCH PRESS

First published in Great Britain 2001

Search Press Limited
Wellwood, North Farm Road,
Tunbridge Wells, Kent TN2 3DR

Reprinted 2004, 2006, 2007

Text copyright © Rosi Robinson 2001

Photographs by Search Press Studios
Photographs and design copyright
© Search Press Ltd. 2001

ISBN10: 0 85532 892 4

ISBN 13: 978 0 85532 892 4

Suppliers

If you have difficulty in obtaining any of the materials and equipment mentioned in this book, then please visit the Search Press website for details of suppliers: www.searchpress.com

Alternatively, you can write to the Publishers at the address above, for a current list of stockists, which includes firms who operate a mail-order service.

Publisher's note

All the step-by-step photographs in this book feature the author, Rosi Robinson, demonstrating how to create batik designs. No models have been used.

Printed in Malaysia by Times Offset (M) Sdn Bhd

In loving memory of my mother Olga Stewart,
a celebrated wild flower artist
and an inspiration for my artistic endeavours.

I would like to thank my husband, Louis, and my children, Laurie and Georgie, for their love and patience over the past year while I have been immersed in wax and dye.

I would also like to thank everyone at Search Press – my editor, John, for his patience and skilful channelling of my enthusiasm, Tamsin, for her imaginative design work, and Lotti, for her excellent photography – I thoroughly enjoyed working with them all.

I would also like to thank all my students, both at school and elsewhere, who have been a constant source of inspiration and encouragement.

Front cover
Rainbow fish

I started this batik by blending a rainbow of colours diagonally across the fabric. I used a canting to wax the fish design, leaving tiny gaps round the fish's scales and other details. Finally, I dipped the whole piece in a dark, black dyebath.

Page 1
Abstract

This colourful batik, created by Rebecca Hall, a ten year old student of mine, shows how exciting wax resists and dyes can be. Rebecca tried out a variety of methods of applying wax, including brushes, home-made stamps and cantings. A canting with two spouts was used to draw the double squiggles.

Page 2-3
Coconut palm

This batik recreates the view I had while lying on a tropical beach. I started the batik by using brushes to wax and dye the tree trunk, then worked the rest of the image by waxing and dip-dyeing, working up from pale yellows to deep greens. The biggest problem with this batik was how to wax the sky areas between the mass of palm leaves.

Opposite
Horse and spray

This is a picture of Disraeli, who belongs to a friend of mine. Every evening, he is taken for a canter along the beach as he loves to splash through the waves. Although his owner was riding him, I used artistic licence to leave her out. I started by waxing all of the horse and concentrated on getting the sea and sky worked up in shades of blue. I then boiled out all the wax, waxed the sea and sky, and worked on the horse.

CONTENTS

Introduction

Like most people, I did some drawing and painting at school but I never felt confident with my artistic skills. As a result, I put art aside and concentrated on academic subjects, reading history at university, then going on to train as a primary school teacher.

However, my teacher training course included an 'Introduction to Art', and a component part of that was batik. The simple idea of wax resisting water (or dye) appealed to me and to my delight, I found that I could use batik to create wonderful designs and colourful patterns. I could control the application of wax with different tools – painting, drawing and spattering it – and I could apply dyes with a brush or by dipping waxed fabric in a dyebath. Batik, I decided, was fun. It was as easy or as difficult as you wanted it to be, and I was hooked!

By a twist of fate, I started my teaching career at a school that had an urgent need for an art specialist. The headmaster decided I should be the 'art specialist'. After all, I *had* taken an 'Introduction to Art' course and attended some 'drawing, painting and batik' evening classes! So along with the usual art lessons, I introduced batik to the children and they took to it immediately. Who would have thought that, thirty years later, I would be Head of Art, teaching batik to children, and writing a book

about it? Perhaps this is proof that all the most important things in life happen by accident.

Since those early days I have taught batik to both adults and children all over Britain. I have visited and lectured in China and Indonesia, learned eastern secrets and shared western ones. Yes, we in the west also have a tradition of batik – we have taken a beautiful art form and made it our own.

A batik design is built up colour by colour, starting with the lighter tints and working through to the darkest, using a sequence of wax, dye, rinse, dry. The process is repeated over and over, building up the many colours you require. Finally, when the design is complete and the wax is removed, what remains is a piece of fabric with your design impregnated into the fibres. The concept of starting with highlights can be confusing at first, but as you progressively wax and dye and the design comes to life, the technique of batik will become easier to comprehend.

Opposite
Flowers and jugs
This picture is a collage of discharged tissue paper. Different colours of tissue paper were placed randomly on the work surface, with some areas overlapping each other. As I brush-waxed the design, the hot wax bonded the sheets together. I painted diluted bleach on the paper, left it to dry, then applied some contrasting dyes over the waxed lines. I did not iron out the wax from this batik. The heat from the iron would have caused residual wax to spread across the paper and create dark halos round each waxed line.

In this book I want you to discover how versatile and adaptable batik is. You do not have to be good at drawing or painting to produce stunning results because the wax, dyes and fabric do a lot of the work for you. The projects in this book are intended to provide a starting point from which you can develop your own ideas. Once you have understood the basic principle that wax and water resist each other, then you will quickly gain confidence to develop the technique further.

'Can I do batik?' is a very common question. My answer is simple, 'If I can, you can!' So let's get started.

Mauritian sunrise

John, my editor, showed me some holiday photographs, and he challenged me to try and reproduce the sunrise as a batik. This is the result. The sky in the photograph was breathtaking, with the rising sun creating some wonderful colour combinations in the clouds, all of which were reflected in the rippling water of the lagoon. I found it rather difficult to capture the pinks next to the turquoise in the sky, but after lots of over-dyeing and the occasional area of discharge, I finally dipped the picture in a dark dyebath.

HISTORY

The term batik first appears in seventeenth-century Dutch texts, and refers to coloured patterned cloth. It is an Indonesian word and derives from the Javanese *ambatik*, which in turn comes from the word *tik* meaning to mark with dots. It was in Java that batik developed into a highly accomplished decorative art form, but the roots of batik go further back in time.

No-one knows precisely when people first applied wax to fabric to resist dye but the craft of batik is at least 2000 years old. Fragments of batik, probably of Indian and Persian origin, have been discovered in ancient Egyptian tombs. It is also known that batik was practised in China as early as 500AD. Thanks to the silk trade it spread across the Far East. In Japan, examples of early eighth-century silk batik screens can be seen in the museum at Nara. And in India there is evidence that batik was done on cotton instead of silk.

It was probably Indian settlers who introduced batik into Java during the twelfth century. It soon became a pastime for fine, aristocratic ladies, and over the next few hundred years it became interwoven with Javanese history and culture. As hand-decorated fabrics for sarongs and other garments became popular, servants were called upon to help in the preparation and dyeing and eventually the waxing of the batik.

In a similar way to the tartan of Scottish clans, distinctive batik designs and dyes made it possible to identify people's rank, status and the area from where they came. By the seventeenth century, batiked cloth in Java had become synonymous with aristocracy and was an integral part of religious celebrations. Batik sarongs, worn by both men and women, became the national costume worn all over Java.

Traditionally, Javanese women, sitting cross-legged on a low stool with a piece of cloth on their laps to catch any drips, waxed the designs on a piece of fabric hung over a wooden frame. The wax was heated in a copper, iron or earthenware pan over an open fire. They used a tool called a canting (originally spelt tjanting) to draw fine lines and dots with hot wax. Cantings have a small copper spout and reservoir fixed to a bamboo or wooden handle. It required great skill to draw with a canting and great care was taken not to spill the wax or touch the fabric whilst drawing. This hand-drawn method is called *tulis* batik, and each piece often took many months to complete.

Detail taken from an early twentieth-century tulis *batik sarong that originates from Pekalongan, on the north coast of Java. A strong Chinese influence is indicated by the inclusion of flowers and animals.*

This Javanese lady is using a canting in the traditional way to create a tulis batik.

When the Dutch colonised Java in the seventeenth century, trade routes opened and Javanese batiks were imported to Holland and other parts of Europe. By the 1830s, batik had become fashionable in Europe, and factories were established in England and Switzerland to produce cheap imitations of hand-printed batiks. However technical problems arose, so the Dutch imported Javanese workers to teach them their techniques. Dutch workers, in turn, were transferred to Indonesia where they supervised the formation of state-controlled co-operatives. But it was not until the late nineteenth and early twentieth centuries, during the Art Nouveau period, that batik became very much in vogue in Holland, Germany and parts of Europe. But as with many other traditional textile processes, these batik skills gradually disappeared, to be replaced by more mechanised production methods such as silk-screening.

NOTE

During the early nineteenth century, when the British ruled Java, Sir Thomas Raffles, the British Lieutenant Governor of Java, set out to learn everything he could about Javanese culture. He was the first to write about the ancient art of batik, and his book, *History of Java*, which he published in 1817, is a most authoritative and exhaustive chronicle of batik methods and patterns. It is one of the most important reference works in the history of batik.

Meanwhile, the men were responsible for preparing the fabric; first rinsing and starching it, then pounding it ready for waxing. When the women had waxed the fabric, the men dyed it in an indigo vat. More wax was added to preserve the blue parts, and some of the original wax was scraped off to allow the next colour, usually soga brown, to penetrate these areas. This process was often repeated many times. Finally, the men boiled out the wax, then ironed the fabric ready for use.

Sometimes the fabric was dewaxed by boiling after every colour, so that the wax did not build up in layers and crack. Traditionally, evidence of cracking was a sign of bad workmanship. However, contemporary Indonesian batik artists use it to good effect, especially for batiks sold to tourists.

This is a detail from a tulis batik that was made in the 1920s. It originates from Yogyakarta, on the south coast of Java, and is dyed with indigo and soga brown.

An intricate Javanese cap

By the mid-nineteenth century, competition from the west had increased to such an extent that the Javanese found it more commercial to mass-produce their batiks as well. They soon developed a method of block printing wax on to fabric using a copper stamp called a cap (originally spelt tjap). The cap consisted of a single motif or design made from copper strips and pins which were soldered on to a copper frame. The cap was pressed on to a wax-soaked pad in a pan of hot wax, held there for a moment, then repeatedly stamped on to the fabric. This method is still used in Java, and over 250 sarongs can be waxed in the time taken to use a canting to draw the same pattern on one piece of fabric.

Following World War Two and the establishment of a Republic of Indonesia, the Javanese batik industry was revitalised. Co-operatives were established for the production of batiks under communal control. The majority of Javanese batiks today are still produced by traditional methods. However there are an increasing number of artists who are adopting a more painterly approach to batik.

Resist dyeing is also practised in many other parts of the world. In Africa, many resists other than wax are used. In Nigeria, cassava-flour paste is applied with cut blocks and stencils to form a resist for indigo-dyed decorative fabric (the Yoruban *adire eleko*). In Senegal

the people use rice paste, while in Mali, the Bambara people apply mud to the fabric and then colour it with a dye from tree bark.

In Japan, starch paste resists made from rice flour are applied through a cone (*tsutsugami*) or stencils (*katazome*).

In India, where the batik industry reached its zenith during the seventeenth and eighteenth centuries, cotton was used instead of silk, and wax drawing was combined with hand-painting.

China also has a long history of resist dyeing, dating back to before 500AD. Today you can find batik being practised by the ethnic people who live on either side of the southwest Chinese border. Here the Miao, Bouyei and Geija people make exquisite batik cloth in combination with embroidery and appliqué. They use different waxing tools to the Javanese and the batiks are predominantly dyed in indigo.

In recent years batik and resist dyeing have become popular in Europe and America. Unlike the Far East where batik is mainly used for clothing, it is now being developed more as an art form. Designs are applied by both traditional and innovative methods on fabric, paper and other materials, and the finished batiks are often framed as paintings or wall hangings.

A cap being used to wax a repeat design. One side of the fabric has already been waxed, and this man is using a matching cap to wax the other side to ensure a perfect resist.

Wax is heated in an old ink pot resting on a bed of hot ashes.

A Bouyei woman from southwest China, applying black wax in a traditional spiral design. When the waxing is complete, the fabric is dipped in indigo dye. Note that the same design appears on the sleeves of her dress.

The finished Bouyei batik after it has been dyed in indigo and dewaxed. The tools used to apply the wax design are different to those used in Java – instead of a cuplike reservoir, these tools hold the wax between a folded metal triangle fitted to a wooden handle.

MATERIALS

Apart from the essentials – fabric or paper, wax and dyes – most of the items you need for batik can be found in the home. You will need a flat, stable work surface, such as a table top, that is near a power point, and you must have access to a sink or water supply.

Fabrics

Fabrics should be smoothly woven, medium-weight, white or light-coloured (the background colour will affect subsequent dyeing) and made from 100% natural fibres.

The dyes I use react only with natural fibres: cotton, linen, silk and wool. The take up of dye colour varies with the weave and fineness of the fibres – dense weaves produce intense colours.

Avoid polycotton and most synthetic materials as these do not take up the dye very well and only washed-out colours will result. Viscose is the only man-made fibre that I have found to give good results.

What you intend doing with your batik will govern the choice of fabric. Silk is ideal for scarves and articles of clothing, whilst cotton and linen are best for pictures, cushion covers, table cloths or wall hangings. Calico, poplin, cotton lawn, rayon, habotai silk, organdie, chiffon, crepe de chine and voile are all suitable for batik.

The type of fabric also affects the absorption of wax. Silk absorbs wax more quickly than cotton, whilst wool (which has a naturally high lanolin content) will take some time to absorb the wax. For thick fabrics, such as canvas or velvet, wax should be applied to both sides to ensure good penetration.

Papers

Any light or medium-weight, thin porous paper can be used for batik. Tissue paper is perfect. Oriental watercolour paper, which is light-weight, yet strong and absorbent, is also a very good material.

Frames

For most projects, especially when applying dye colours, it is best to stretch the fabric on a frame to keep it raised above the work surface. Various types of frame are available.

Special, adjustable batik frames can be bought from craft shops. These are useful but they can be expensive.

Artists' stretchers (for stretching canvas) are a good alternative. They are available in many sizes, they are made of soft wood (they accept pins easily) and they can be dismantled for storage or transportation.

Old picture frames can also be used. However, these are often made from wood which is too hard to accept pins. Embroidery or rug-hooking frames on stands are also ideal for batik.

You can make your own wooden frame by joining four lengths of 25 x 50mm (1 x 2 in) soft wood together. Nail or screw the corners together, then sand them smooth.

Whatever type of frame you choose, always cover the working side of the frame with masking or plastic parcel tape. After each dyeing, this surface can be wiped clean to prevent excess dye from staining the new piece of cloth.

You will need some pins to stretch the fabric on the frame. Three-pronged silk pins are ideal, but ordinary drawing pins work just as well. When working with silk scarves, where you need to dye right up to the edge, you can use special stenter pins.

Waxing equipment

WAX

For most of the projects in this book I use batik wax which is a very versatile, ready-blended combination of hard and soft wax. However, you can make up your own blends (see page 22), and a few words about the characteristics of beeswax, microcrystalline wax (a synthetic beeswax) and paraffin wax may prove helpful.

Beeswax is excellent for drawing lines and fine details. It is soft and pliable, and resists cracking.

Microcrystalline wax is cheaper than pure beeswax but has the same qualities of softness and pliability.

Paraffin wax is a hard and brittle wax that has poor adhesive properties if used on its own. It cracks easily, and it can flake and peel off the fabric.

You can also achieve batik effects with cold wax, in the form of candles, oil pastels and wax crayons. These are ideal for drawing and rubbing designs on fabrics, but as cold wax does not penetrate the surface, dip-dyeing is not advised.

Cold resin, gutta and paste resists can also be used for resist work. Although I have not used any of these in this book they are worthy of mention. When you are familiar with the properties of the normal wax resists, you may want to experiment with them.

WAX POT

Wax must be melted before you apply it, and the safest and most efficient means of heating it is in a thermostatically-controlled wax pot.

For stamp waxing you need a wide, shallow wax pot – an old electric frying pan is ideal (see page 22).

You could stand a wax container in a large pan of hot water – similar to a double boiler or bain-marie – but you must keep the water level topped up, and avoid dropping water in the hot wax.

Wax is flammable, so never heat wax directly over an open flame or an electric burner.

WAX BRUSHES

Choose good quality, stiff, natural bristle brushes. Soft-haired ones may become spiky or lose their bristles easily, while synthetic bristles can melt in the hot wax.

Flat or wide brushes are good for filling in large areas quickly and effectively, for creating a sense of movement, and for spattering. Oriental, round, fine pointed brushes hold a lot of wax and are good for most applications: outlines, dots, thin and thick lines, and for filling in. Household paintbrushes are useful for broad strokes, and they can be trimmed to different shapes.

It is difficult to remove wax from brushes (unless you clean them with white spirit), so they are best kept just for waxing. Bristles become stiff when the wax solidifies, but they soften up again when dipped in hot wax.

CANTINGS

Cantings (or tjantings) are the traditional Javanese tools for drawing fine lines and dots of wax. Usually, they have a brass or copper reservoir and spout attached to a wooden handle. The hot wax flows through the spout, and the size of the spout controls the width of line. Some cantings have double or triple spouts.

Indonesian and western designs of canting are available from craft suppliers. Similar tools, called kystkas (used by Ukranians for decorating eggs) are also excellent for drawing fine lines. I prefer to use Indonesian style cantings, and kystkas.

You can buy temperature-controlled, electric cantings. However, these tools are usually quite heavy and rather cumbersome to use.

STAMPS OR CAPS (TJAPS)

Stamps (or caps) can be used for applying wax on to fabric rather like a printing block. While traditional Indonesian caps have very intricate patterns, you can create some very effective designs by stamping with common household objects (see page 36).

OTHER TOOLS

Meat skewers, **blunt nails** and **darning needles** make good tools for etching fine detail into wax.

Masking tape and **adhesive stencil paper** can be used as masks to control the application of wax.

An old **iron** (non-steam) and plenty of clean **newsprint** are useful for removing most of the wax from the finished batik.

Paper towel is ideal for catching drips from cantings, and for stamping textured waxed resists.

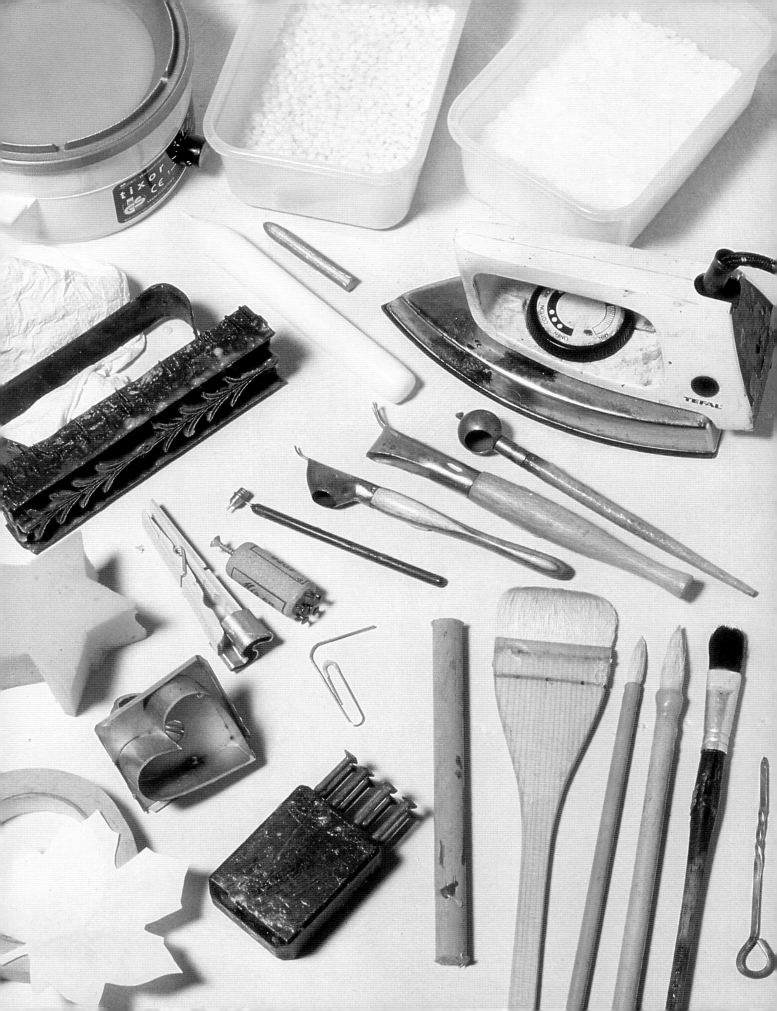

Dyeing equipment

DYES

I use Procion MX cold water, fibre-reactive dyes, as they can be used with a wide range of fabrics and papers. They are available in a full spectrum of intermixable colours and are activated/fixed by adding an alkali fixing agent, which makes them extremely colourfast and washable. The dyes are ideal for batik as they can be used for direct application as well as for dip-dyeing. Most brands of dye come in powder form, which will keep almost indefinitely in an airtight container in a cool dry place.

Natural dyes such as indigo are also ideal for batik. Cold water direct dyes can be used, but they are less versatile.

CHEMICALS

Sodium carbonate is an alkali fixing agent used to bond the dyes to the fibres of the fabric. It is available in the form of soda ash or washing soda.

Urea is a wetting agent, which is made up into chemical water (see page 23). Chemical water is used to make up stock dyes for direct application, and helps keep the applied dyes wet long enough for them to penetrate the fibres and produce bright colours.

Sodium alginate is used to thicken directly-applied dyes, to restrict their free-flowing characteristics, and is added to chemical water (see page 23).

Bleach is used to remove (discharge) colour from dyed fabrics and papers (see page 76). Never use bleach on silk as it rots the fibres.

Distilled white vinegar (or acetic acid) is used as a neutraliser for bleach when using the discharging technique.

Salt is a levelling agent that is added to a dyebath when dip-dyeing. It has an electrostatic charge that pushes dye through the water on to the fabric, and helps produce even colour. Non-iodized table salt is preferred but not absolutely necessary.

Salt can also be sprinkled on to still-wet dyes to create interesting textures and patterns (see page 70). The size of crystals affects the result, so experiment with different types (coarse sea salt, table salt and dishwasher salt).

DYE BRUSHES AND APPLICATORS

You can use a variety of brushes for applying dyes. I like to use oriental watercolour brushes for general painting – they hold a lot of dye and have a good point – but normal round watercolour brushes work equally well. Wide sponge or wallpaper brushes are ideal for laying washes over large areas of fabric. For spattering colour, I tap a loaded brush against a wooden stick. You can also apply dye through small spray bottles or plant misters.

JARS, SYRINGES AND PALETTES

You will need quite a few jars for mixing and storing dyes and chemicals. You will also need a jar of clean water for rinsing brushes. Syringes or droppers are ideal for transferring dyes from the jars to the palette. Deep-welled palettes are the most useful type for mixing dyes.

MEASURING EQUIPMENT

You will need a measuring jug and a selection of spoons for making up the dyes and chemicals. Always take notes about the precise amounts used for batches of dyes so that you can compare results. A small weighing machine may prove useful.

DYEBATHS

Dyebaths are used for dip-dyeing, and should be large enough to allow the fabric to be completely immersed and move freely. Large shallow containers often work better than tall narrow ones. Plastic, glass, stainless steel or enamel containers are all suitable. Do not use copper, aluminium, iron or galvanised containers.

Other equipment

Most dyes are very fine powders, so a filter-type **face mask** must be used when mixing them. To protect your hands and clothing, always wear **rubber gloves** and an **apron** or **overall** when dyeing.

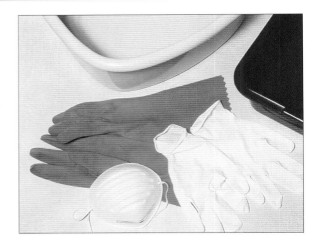

You will need plenty of **newsprint** or old **newspapers** for covering the work surface. **Newsprint** is also used when ironing out wax from the finished batik.

Waxed shelf paper can be used as the top layer on your work surface to inhibit adhesion of wax.

Use strong **plastic sheeting** to protect your work surface. An old **blanket**, placed under the plastic sheet, provides the necessary 'give' required when waxing with stamps. You might also consider placing some plastic sheeting on the floor.

A good supply of **paper towel** is essential for mopping up spills.

I occasionally use a **hairdryer** to dry dyes.

Use a **water-soluble marker pen** or **soft pencil** to draw designs on white or pale coloured fabrics. Use white or coloured **carbon paper** to transfer designs on to dark fabrics.

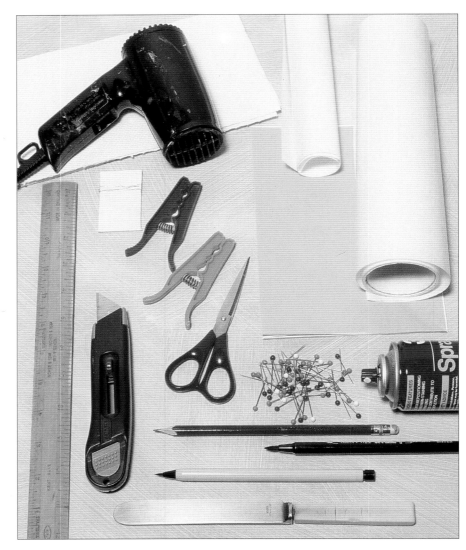

A **craft knife** and a pair of **scissors** are always useful.

Always use **plastic pegs** and a plastic covered **washing line** to hang the finished batiks while they are drying.

Fine **fuse wire** can be used to clean the spouts on cantings.

Spray adhesive is ideal for mounting finished paper batiks on to card. You can purchase special, **acid-free self-adhesive card** for mounting fabric batiks.

Dressmakers' pins are used to pin paper patterns to fabric.

GETTING STARTED

The working area

Batik can be rather messy, so work in a well-lit and well-ventilated space, preferably away from your main living area, where spills of dyes and wax will not cause a problem. The space should be large enough to have a flat, stable working surface. You will also need access to power supply points for the wax pot, hairdryer and iron, and a sink or a water supply.

Cover the work surface with heavy plastic sheeting and plenty of newsprint or newspaper. When waxing, you could use waxed shelf paper to minimise adhesion of the hot wax. For stamp waxing the work surface should have some 'give' in it – place an old blanket under the plastic to make a simple printing bed. I would also suggest that you place plastic sheeting on the floor to protect it against spills of dye.

You will also need a drying line, or a flat surface, away from direct sunlight, where the dyed fabrics can dry naturally.

Here, I am preparing to stamp wax so I have placed on old blanket under the plastic.

Preparing the fabric

Fabrics are often treated with a special finish (dressing) which makes them water-resistant and less absorbent, and this must be removed before you start batik work. Wash the fabric with a mild detergent, rinse it and squeeze out excess water, then while it is still damp, press it with an iron. Handwash delicate fabrics in lukewarm water with soap flakes.

If you intend to apply dyes directly to the fabric, you can pretreat the fabric with a fix solution (see opposite). Thoroughly soak the fabric in the fix solution for ten minutes, then squeeze out excess liquid, dry it and press it with a cool iron. Alternatively, you can stretch the fabric on a frame, paint on the fix solution and leave it to dry before applying wax or dyes. If you intend to apply more than two layers of dye, paint more fix on to the fabric after every two layers.

When stretching fabric on a frame, try to keep the weave structure parallel to the sides of the frame. Start by pinning one corner, then, stretching the fabric along the grain, pin up the sides. Adjust the pins to create even tension across the fabric so that it is smooth and flat. If the fabric is larger than the frame, stretch, wax and dye the design section by section.

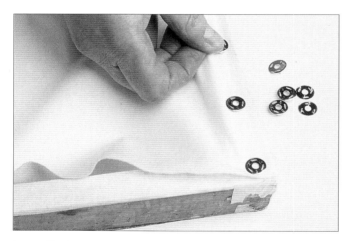

I use silk pins to stretch the fabric on a frame covered with masking tape.

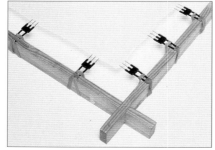

When I want to work right up to the edge of, say, a piece of silk, I use stenter pins.

Preparing the wax

Batik wax will prove suitable for most projects, but it is worth trying out other blends. A blend of 50% beeswax and 50% paraffin wax is a good starting point, and this mix provides a good resist and reasonable cracks. If you want lots of cracks, increase the proportion of hard, paraffin wax. On the other hand, if you really want to restrict cracks, increase the proportion of soft beeswax. Another common blend is one-third each of beeswax, microcrystalline wax and paraffin wax.

The required temperature of the hot wax will vary with different fabrics, but is usually between 120 and 140°C (250 and 285°F). As a general rule, the wax must be just hot enough to penetrate the fabric on application and it should appear transparent on contact. If it is not hot enough, the wax will appear milky and opaque on contact with the fabric. It will not penetrate the fabric satisfactorily and it may flake off, allowing dye to bleed under. On the other hand, if the wax is too hot, it starts to smoke. It also becomes so fluid that it will not penetrate the material properly, and may froth on contact with the fabric.

A flat shallow container, such as the electric frying pan below, is best for waxing with stamps. Place a block of felt wadding or a flat kitchen scourer in the pan to act as a stamp pad. The melted wax should just cover the pad, as an overloaded stamp will produce poor images.

A large shallow wax pot is best for waxing with stamps. The rocks in this old electric frying pan are used to support cantings.

Preparing wax brushes

Dipping new brushes in hot wax will cause them to fuzz out, and it may take some time to remove all the trapped air. Overcome this problem by dipping them into the wax pot while the wax is heating up, gradually immersing the bristles into the wax until all air has been dispelled. Create a point on a waxed brush by wiping the bristles on the side of the wax pot. By the time the wax reaches its operating temperature the brush will be fully loaded.

Gradually immerse new bristles into the wax.

Wipe the bristles on the side of the wax pot to create a point.

SAFETY NOTES

Wax is flammable, so treat it with respect and ensure that it does not overheat. When the wax becomes too hot, it starts to smoke.

- Never leave the room without turning off the heat source.
- In the unlikely event of fire, snuff out the flames with a cover or lid — never use water.
- Wax pots become hot, so do not touch them.
- If hot wax is spilled on your skin, run it under cold water, then peel off the wax.
- Never re-use wax that has been removed from a finished batik — it may splutter when reheated.
- Never leave brushes in the wax pot as they will lose their shape and may also lose their bristles.

Mixing chemicals

There are no hard and fast rules about mixing the chemicals and dyes — every batik artist has their own methods and short-cuts — so treat these recipes as a starting point for your own experiments.

Chemical water   This is only used for dye painting. Thoroughly dissolve four tablespoons of urea in one litre (two pints) of warm water, then leave to cool. Store in an airtight container, at room temperature for up to six months. If you live in a hard-water area, add one teaspoon of water softener to the urea before adding the water.

Thick chemical water   Slowly sprinkle two or three teaspoons of thickener (sodium alginate) over one litre (two pints) of chemical water, then whisk or liquidise until smooth. Leave to stand for one hour, stir again, then leave it overnight before using. This can be stored for up to a month in an airtight container in a cool, dark place or in a refrigerator.

Fix solution   Dyes need an alkali fixing agent to make them bond to the fibres. For direct dyeing applications, you can either pretreat the fabric with the fix solution or add the fix to the dyes themselves. When dip-dyeing, the fix is added to the dyebath during the dipping process.

Thoroughly dissolve two heaped teaspoons of soda ash in a little hot water, then top up to one litre (two pints) with cold water. The solution can be stored at room temperature. For dipping, use two heaped teaspoons of soda ash per litre (two pints) of dyebath.

Neutralising bath   This is used when bleaching cotton. Mix three tablespoons of distilled white vinegar, or one tablespoon of acetic acid in one litre (two pints) of cold water.

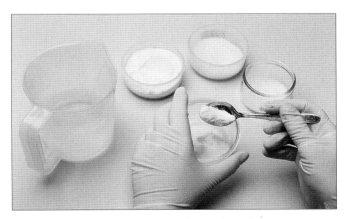

Always wear gloves when mixing chemicals and dyes.

Preparing dyes

There are two basic methods for applying dye colour: direct application, where the dye is hand-painted on to the fabric with a brush, sponge or spray bottle; and dip-dyeing, where successive colours are applied by immersing the fabric in a dyebath. You can work a design entirely in one method or you can combine them. The method of application governs the way in which the dyes are prepared.

DYE PAINTING

Before starting a batik, prepare 250ml (half pint) solutions of each dye colour you intend to use by mixing dye powder with chemical water (see page 23). You can vary the ratio of dye colour to chemical water to produce a range of shades:

- half to one level teaspoon of dye for a pale shade
- two to three level teaspoons of dye for a medium shade
- five or more teaspoons of dye for a dark shade

To make each solution, measure the dye powder into a small container, make it into a paste with a little chemical water, then, stirring continuously, gradually add more chemical water to make up 250ml (half a pint) of solution. Transfer the solution into glass or plastic airtight jars and label them with the amount of colour used and the date. These can be stored for up to five days at room temperature. These dye solutions can be applied directly on to fabrics that have been pretreated with the fix solution.

If you want to work on untreated fabric, you must make up the dye solution using chemical water and the fix solution. These dyes only remain stable for two or three hours and they cannot be stored, so mix them just prior to starting a batik. Mix the dye powder into a paste with three tablespoons of chemical water, then top up to 250ml (half a pint) using 50% chemical water and 50% fix solution.

If you want to use thick dyes, make up smaller quantities in a palette, using tiny amounts of dye powder. Mix with thick chemical water when working on pretreated fabric. Mix with a 50:50 mix of thick chemical water and fix solution when working on untreated fabrics.

Add dry dye powder to a little chemical water and mix to a paste.

Top up with more chemical water to make batches of 250ml (half a pint).

SAFTETY NOTES

- Always wear rubber gloves and an overall when working with dyes.
- Always wear a face mask to avoid breathing in dye powders.
- Do not eat, drink or smoke in the dyeing area.
- Equipment must be reserved for use with dyes and nothing else.
- Clearly label containers for dyes and chemicals.
- Never use hot water with dye powders, as it will melt the wax.
- Make sure there is adequate ventilation.

DIP-DYEING

In contrast to the direct application of dyes, dip-dyeing requires the fabric to be fully submerged in a large volume of a weaker dye solution. Salt is added to the dye solution to drive the dye into the fibres and achieve a uniform spread of colour. The longer the fabric is immersed, the greater will be the take up of colour. The fix solution is then added to the dyebath to fix the dye in the fibres.

The total quantity of water used in a dyebath must be sufficient to cover the fabric to be dyed. A three litre (six pint) dyebath will be sufficient for up to 100g (3oz) of cotton – about 1.5m² (1.8yd²) of fabric.

Mix the dye powder into a paste with a small amount of warm water, add more water to make a concentrated solution, then add this solution to the dyebath. For a three-litre dyebath use, say, half a teaspoon of dye powder for pale shades, one teaspoon for mid shades, and two teaspoons for dark ones.

Finally, add the salt to the dyebath. The quantity required depends on the volume of water and the quantity of dye powder used. Use two heaped teaspoons per litre (two pints) of dyebath for light shades, four heaped teaspoons per litre (two pints) for mid shades and six heaped teaspoons per litre (two pints) for dark shades. Now you are ready to dip-dye the fabric.

The activator/fix solution is not added until halfway through the dyeing process (see page 46).

Add concentrated dye solution to the dyebath.

Final removal of wax

After dyeing and drying, wax should be removed from the finished batik.

You can remove most of the wax from paper and fabrics by ironing. Place the batik on a good layer of clean newsprint, then place a single sheet on top. Iron over the top sheet of paper with a hot iron, pressing down as you work across it. The heat of the iron pulls the wax from the fabric into the paper. Change the papers on each side of the fabric as they become saturated with wax. Remove the paper while the wax is still molten so that the paper does not stick to the fabric. Try not to press wrinkles in the hot, waxy fabric as these can be difficult to remove later.

It is impossible to remove all traces of wax by ironing, so if you want a wax-free batik, have the batik dry-cleaned.

If you are sure that the dyes are fixed properly, then you can remove wax from all fabrics except silk, by boiling them in hot water (see page 73). Wax removed by boiling must never be re-used.

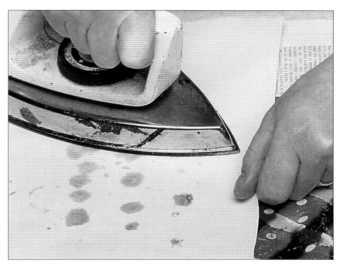

Change the paper regularly when ironing out wax.

Understanding colour

Colour is the most important and exciting element of batik. The way that colours spread and blend on the fabric is almost magical. Dye colours are transparent, so new colours can be created by overlaying one colour on another on the fabric, or by mixing dyes in a palette. Colours you want to keep must be covered with wax, before applying more dye.

There is a wide range of ready-mixed dye colours available, but two yellows, two reds, two blues and a few darks will be sufficient to get you started. I used just the following dyes for all the projects in this book:

- yellows: lemon yellow and golden yellow
- reds: scarlet and cerise
- blues: turquoise and royal blue
- darks: mahogany, navy blue and/or black

The yellows, reds and blues were used to create the colour chart opposite. I dyed horizontal stripes first, waxed some marks on these, over-dyed vertical stripes using the same colours, then removed the wax. Apart from the wide range of colours created, note the different hues in the blocks where a colour is overlaid on itself.

The colour wheel below shows that these same six colours can be mixed to create 'true' primary colours and secondary colours (green, purple and orange).

You can create a wonderful range of browns and greys by mixing complementary colours together. Complementary colours are diametrically opposite each other on the colour wheel. Neat dyes are rather bright, and they can be dulled or darkened by mixing small amounts of complementary colours. For really dark tones add small amounts of navy blue or black.

Colours always appear darker when wet, so always test colour mixtures on scraps of the same fabric used for the project.

Look closely at your chosen subject and notice how light affects the colours. Try to visualise texture – tree bark, flaky paint, sparkles on water – as layers of colours. Think about how can you create these effects in batik, working from the lightest tones to the darkest. At first you may find this confusing, but as you become more familiar with the process, your eye will begin to discern the combination and layering of colour required for a specific effect. Soon you will learn to anticipate the over-dyeing sequences and be more aware of the appropriate tool or technique to use.

Dyes are transparent and intermixable. Use dropper bottles to transfer dyes to the palette, then mix them together with a brush. Dilute colours with chemical water.

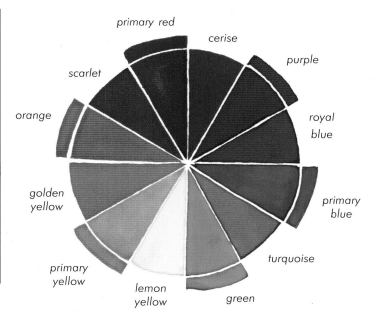

This colour wheel was dyed using the yellows, reds and blues listed above.

Techniques

The batik processes and projects in this section are a guide to get you started. I introduce you to traditional and new batik techniques, starting with the making of simple marks or patterns with the wax, then going on to drawing with a brush and a canting.

You do not need to be able to draw – where appropriate I have included outline sketches for you to use – and at the beginning of each project, I have included a list of the tools and materials you need. The tools are easy to handle, but I suggest that you experiment with them on fabric remnants before you start any of the projects. Before you begin a project, wash and pre-soak the fabric, prepare your working area, and make sure you have everything at hand.

As you work through the projects, you will become more proficient in handling the waxes, tools and dyes, and will become more confident with your designs and pictures. As you expand your range of techniques you will discover many possibilities for interpreting texture and movement. Soon you will evolve your own manner of working. By the time you have tried all the techniques you should have a much better understanding of what batik is. If you are not hooked by then, I will have somehow failed!

USING HARD WAX

The easiest way to create a waxed design on
paper or fabric is with hard, cold wax in the form
of candles, crayons or oil pastels. You can draw a
design straight on to paper or fabric, you can rub
a design through from a textured surface (much
like brass rubbing) or you can drip spots or trails
of melted wax from a lighted candle on the
surface. The waxed areas of the paper or fabric
resist the dye, and only the unwaxed areas will
take up the applied colour. The rubbing technique
is very versatile – coins, leaves, tree bark, bricks,
floorboards and gratings are just a few of the
everyday surfaces you could try.

Abstract book cover

In this first project I show you how to make a colourful sheet of paper for a book cover. I use a candle and an oil pastel to create wax resists and just three dye colours. You could use the same waxing techniques to cover a lampshade or a box, or you could include them as part of a multi-technique project.

Before you start the project, you must measure your book to determine the overall size of paper necessary to cover it. Remember to allow for flaps at the top, bottom and sides of the covers. I have used a light-weight, oriental watercolour paper, which is thin yet extremely strong, and absorbs dye colours well. A good alternative is tissue paper or absorbent banqueting roll.

YOU WILL NEED

Book to be covered

Light-weight oriental watercolour paper

Scissors

White candle and matches

Gold oil pastel

Textured surface (trivet)

Dye colours: lemon yellow, scarlet and turquoise

Dye brushes

Hairdryer

Craft knife and flat-bladed knife

Iron and ironing board

Spray adhesive

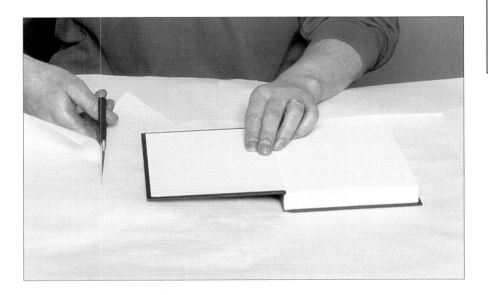

1 Using the book as a guide, and allowing for turn-ins all round, cut a sheet of white watercolour paper to size.

2 Drop spots of melted wax from a lighted candle in columns across the paper.

NOTE

Drawn and rubbed wax resists tend to sit on the surface, and not penetrate right through the paper or fabric. Adding thickener to the dye colours (see page 18) will help stop dye colours running through the resist.

4 Use a hairdryer to dry the paper. Take care to ensure that the heat does not melt the wax.

3 Use a large dye brush to apply diagonal stripes of lemon yellow dye across the sheet then, while the yellow is still damp, apply stripes of scarlet on the opposite diagonal.

5 Use a craft knife to 'sharpen' the candle.

6 Use the candle to apply small circles of wax over all the intersections of the lemon yellow and scarlet stripes.

7 Place the paper face up on the textured surface of the trivet, then gently rub a gold oil pastel across the surface to create a random pattern.

NOTE

Rubbing texture on to paper is quite easy. However, when rubbing on to fabric, you must ensure that the fabric is stretched taut over the textured surface.

8 Use a sponge brush to apply diagonal stripes of turquoise right across the paper. Leave to dry naturally, or use a hairdryer to speed up the process.

9 Use the tip of a flat-bladed knife or spatula to prize off heavy deposits of wax.

10 Protect your ironing surface with a thick layer of newspapers. Sandwich the decorated paper between sheets of newspaper or newsprint and iron out the wax. Change the paper frequently until there are no signs of wax being removed.

11 Apply a coat of spray adhesive on the back of the paper.

12 Wrap the paper round the book, mitre the corners and turn in the end flaps. Trim excess paper at the top and bottom of the spine then turn in the top and bottom flaps.

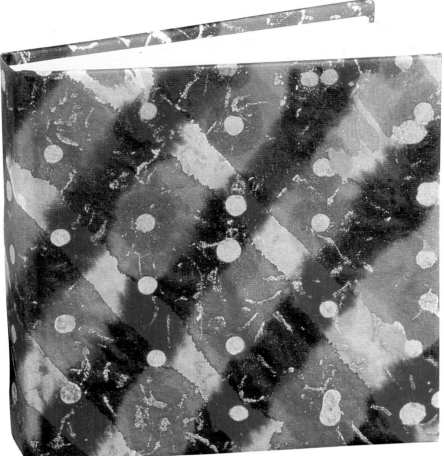

The finished book cover

Although I used cold wax resists for this project, you can produce similar effects with the other waxing techniques included in this book.

Covered box

White tissue paper was first dyed with red and blue stripes. Then, using similar techniques to those for the book cover above, the paper was waxed and decorated with other colours.

'Blank' boxes, suitable for covering in this way, are readily available from craft shops.

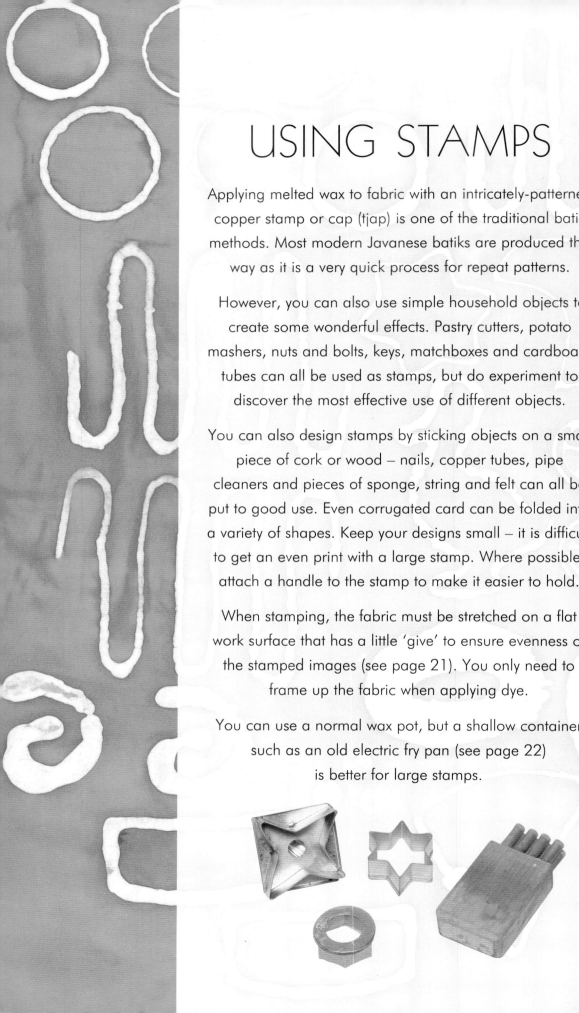

USING STAMPS

Applying melted wax to fabric with an intricately-patterned copper stamp or cap (tjap) is one of the traditional batik methods. Most modern Javanese batiks are produced this way as it is a very quick process for repeat patterns.

However, you can also use simple household objects to create some wonderful effects. Pastry cutters, potato mashers, nuts and bolts, keys, matchboxes and cardboard tubes can all be used as stamps, but do experiment to discover the most effective use of different objects.

You can also design stamps by sticking objects on a small piece of cork or wood – nails, copper tubes, pipe cleaners and pieces of sponge, string and felt can all be put to good use. Even corrugated card can be folded into a variety of shapes. Keep your designs small – it is difficult to get an even print with a large stamp. Where possible, attach a handle to the stamp to make it easier to hold.

When stamping, the fabric must be stretched on a flat work surface that has a little 'give' to ensure evenness of the stamped images (see page 21). You only need to frame up the fabric when applying dye.

You can use a normal wax pot, but a shallow container such as an old electric fry pan (see page 22) is better for large stamps.

Simple landscape cushion cover

In this project, I show you how to create a simple landscape scene using a range of simple, home-made stamps and three colour dyes. The subject is easy to adapt depending on the stamps you have available. The design in itself is not too complicated as I want to show that it is possible to use wax and dyes in a free and imaginative way. Sometimes the medium takes over and unplanned effects happen. For example when wet dye meets a dry surface it often forms hard edges. These 'accidents' can create some exciting effects that can be incorporated into the design.

YOU WILL NEED

Untreated cotton fabric (see page 22)

Soft pencil

Batik wax and wax pot

Home-made stamps:
Paper towel, wooden ruler, folded-cardboard shapes, large and small paperclips, bottle cork with five brads pushed into one end, corrugated card

Masking tape

Frame and pins

Fixed dye colours: lemon yellow, scarlet, turquoise

Dye brushes

1 Use a soft pencil to transfer the design on to the fabric, then stretch the fabric on the prepared work surface (see page 22).

2 Scrunch up a paper towel, dip it in the wax and scrape it on the side of the pot to remove excess wax.

NOTE

When stamping wax resists, you must work fairly rapidly so the stamp does not cool.

Hold the stamp in the hot wax for a few seconds and allow to heat up. Then, working quickly, lift the stamp out of the pot, shake off excess wax, gently touch it on to a piece of paper, then press the stamp firmly on the fabric. Lift the stamp off the fabric, recharge it with wax, then make another waxed image.

Stamped wax often adheres to the work surface, so when you have finished each stamping, carefully pull the fabric away from the work surface.

3 Lightly dab the waxed paper towel across the sky area to create clouds. Recharge the towel with wax as you work across the fabric. Hold the fabric up to a light to check your progress. Make a tiny ball of paper towel and use this to create smaller areas of texture across the middle distant field.

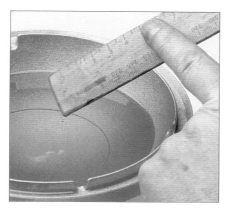

4 Dip the end of the ruler in the wax, then tap the ruler to remove excess wax. Wood is not a good conductor of heat, so work quickly.

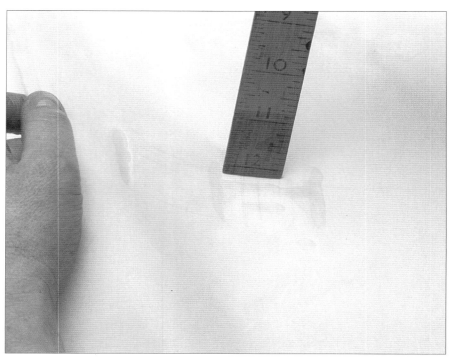

5 Stamp the end of the ruler on the fabric to create a fence post. Continue recharging the ruler and stamping shapes to build up the fence and gate.

6 Fold strips of card to form stamps for the outlines of the church and the gravestones, then secure each shape with masking tape. Dip the end of the card stamp in the melted wax. Do not worry if bubbles start to form when a card stamp is first introduced to the melted wax – this is quite normal, and the bubbles will not last long.

7 Stamp these shapes on to the fabric to build up the outlines for the church, its spire and the gravestones.

8 Stretch and pin the fabric to a frame, then use a wide foam sponge brush and chemical water to dampen the fabric.

9 Apply a pale turquoise wash across the sky. While the fabric is still damp, apply a lemon yellow wash across the rest of the fabric and allow the two colours to merge together just below horizon. Note how the waxed clouds and the texture in the field become very visible.

10 Use a small round brush and scarlet dye to drop small spots of colour on to the damp yellow foreground to suggest poppy heads. Do not load too much dye on the brush, as the dye will spread quite quickly. Then, working round the scarlet poppies, add more yellow across the foreground.

NOTE

If you want to add detail without the colour spreading, add a thickener to the dye (see page 24).

11 Apply bands of turquoise dye into the damp middle distant yellow area. Notice how it spreads across the fabric until it is stopped by the wax resist at the skyline and the fence. Leave to dry.

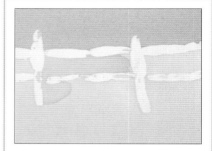

NOTE

Do not be alarmed if, as shown in the detail above, colour bleeds through a gap in the wax resist. You could stop the flow by drying the fabric with a hairdryer and plugging the gap with wax. However, here it did not matter, and the 'dry line' will be rectified later.

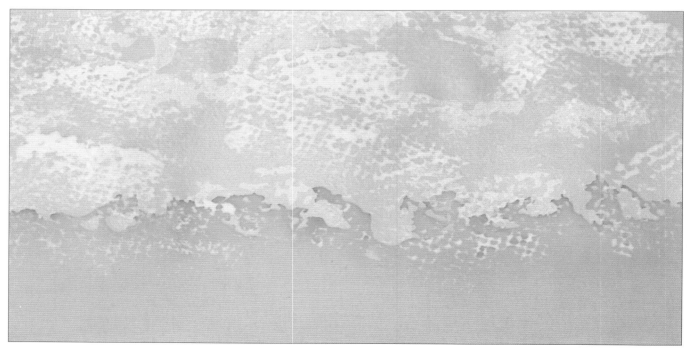

12 Scrunch up another paper towel to work more wax along the skyline. Apply more turquoise dye into the middle distant field, then allow the fabric to dry naturally. Note the lovely hard-edged tree shapes that appear when the dye is stopped by the wax and the areas of dried dye along the skyline.

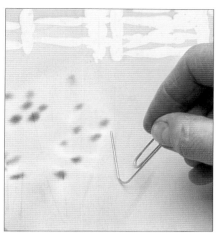

13 Hold a large paperclip in the wax pot to warm up, dab off excess wax on a paper towel, then use the paperclip to wax grasses and flower stems over the foreground. Use a small clip to make the finer blades of grass close to the fence, and to outline the track from the gate to the church.

14 Use the cork/nailhead stamp to wax small spots around the red flower heads.

15 Use a scrunched up paper towel to wax texture into the foreground and into the area just below the distant tree/ sky line.

16 Use rolled-up corrugated card to create texture over the middle distant fields. Again, do not worry about any bubbles that appear in the wax pot.

17 Apply various tones of turquoise (wet on dry) across the middle distant and foreground grasses. Mix all three colours to make brown, and colour the church. Use the same mix and subtle variations of it to add detail to the distant trees, the track and the bottom of the fence posts.

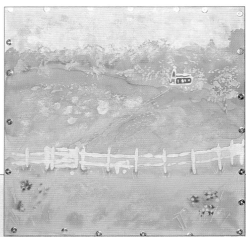

18 Leave the finished batik to fix on its frame, by allowing it to dry naturally overnight, preferably in a moist atmosphere. Remove the dried batik from the frame, rinse off any excess dye, leave to dry, then iron out as much wax as possible (see page 25). If you want to remove all the wax, take the batik to a dry-cleaner.

The finished batik after removing the wax. Notice how the image has become much sharper and brighter.

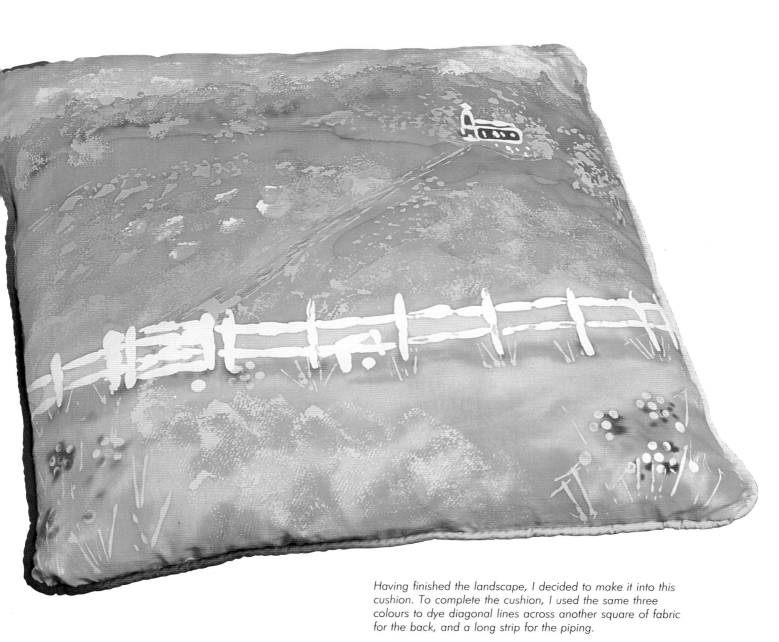

Having finished the landscape, I decided to make it into this cushion. To complete the cushion, I used the same three colours to dye diagonal lines across another square of fabric for the back, and a long strip for the piping.

USING BRUSHES

A brush is an excellent and versatile waxing tool for drawing and it can be used to create a variety of waxed effects. You can use a brush for filling in large areas, for making dots and lines and for spattered and stippled effects. You can also achieve a feathered effect by lifting the brush at the end of each short stroke.

Experiment by waxing on scrap pieces of fabric. Do not overload the brush with wax. Vary the speed and pressure of brush strokes and note how these affect the flow and penetration of wax. The wax on the brush cools quite quickly so you will have to recharge the brush after every stroke to ensure that the wax penetrates the fabric on first impact. The wax should appear clear or transparent as it penetrates the fabric. If it looks milky or opaque, it is not hot enough.

You may find it easier to use a small brush to outline areas and then fill them in with a large one. When the hot wax touches the fabric, it has a tendency to spread as well as penetrate. This means you must keep the brush moving or a sizeable dot or blob will result. At first you may find the wax difficult to control – it may overrun lines – but with experience you will learn to work the brush just inside a drawn line to allow for this.

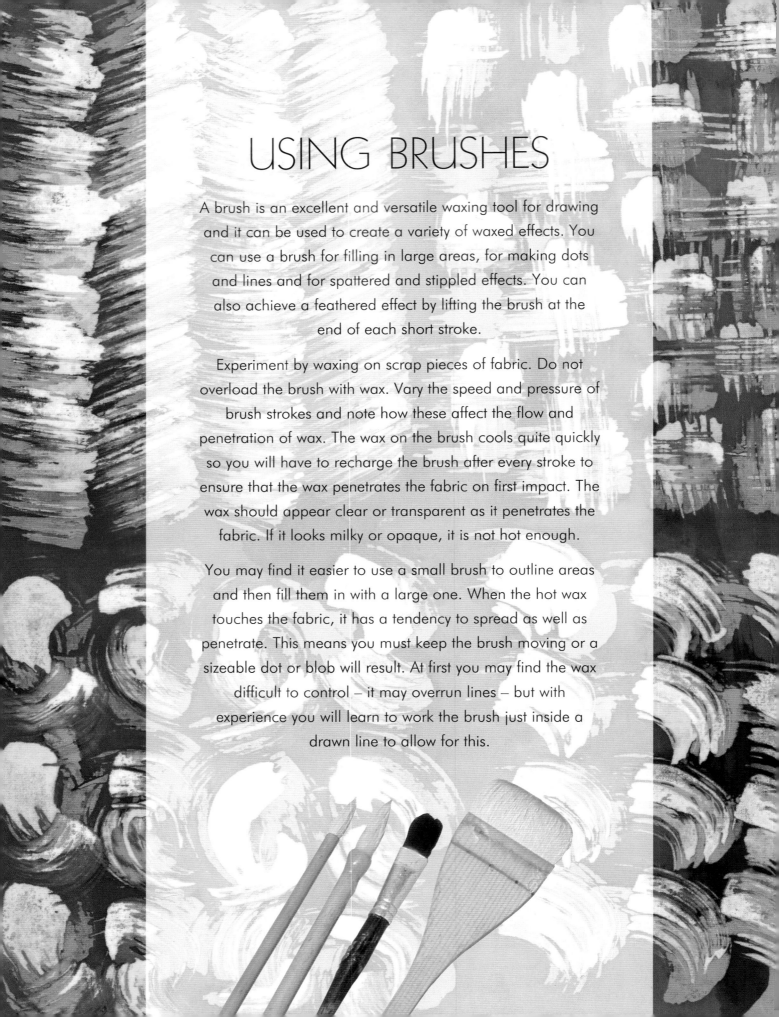

Leaf scarf

In this project I show you how to create a stunning silk scarf. I use two basic methods of applying wax with a brush. In the first, wax is feathered over strips of masking tape to create a border. In the second, a loaded brush is tapped against a wooden stick to spatter droplets of wax over the background, some of which is masked with a leaf shape.

I also introduce the technique of dip-dyeing to produce uniform colour in all the unwaxed areas of the fabric. Just two colours are used for this project, but you can include as many as you wish. Always start with the lightest colour and work up to the darkest, remembering that unwaxed areas will take up all the applied dyes.

Design sketch.

Detail of leaf mask. Enlarge this design to your required size, trace it on to sticky-backed stencil paper, then cut round the outline. Make five masks.

YOU WILL NEED

White silk scarf with rolled edges

Wax brushes: a wide one for spattering; a flat one for feathering; and a small pointed one for drawing lines.

Wooden stick or ruler for spattering

Batik wax and wax pot

Prepared dyebaths (see page 25): turquoise and royal blue

Fix solution (see page 23)

Rubber gloves

Masking tape and sticky-backed stencil paper

Scissors

NOTE

When you have finished waxing, do not lay the wax brushes directly on a hard surface.

Never bend wax-hardened bristles as you could break them.

Keep dye brushes away from the wax pot!

1 Wash and press the scarf to remove any creases. Stretch the scarf flat on the work surface, then stick on long strips of masking tape as shown in the design sketch. These strips create a wax-free, straight-edged border.

2 Use the flat wax brush to 'feather' wax at right angles to the strips of masking tape. You do not need much wax on the brush, so scrape off excess wax on the side of the pot. Work quickly, making a series of short brush strokes, pressing the brush down on to the masking tape and lifting it up as you wax on to the silk. Wax both sides of each strip.

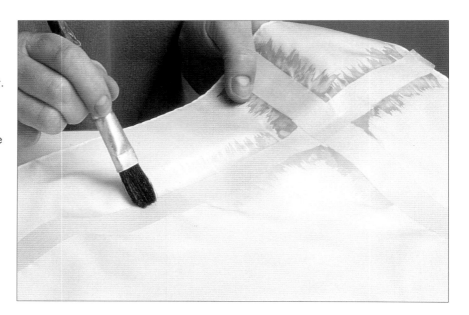

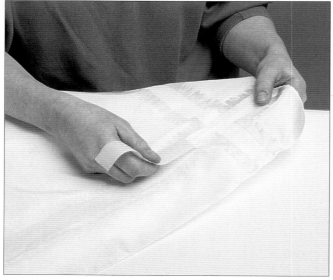

3 When you have waxed all four lengths of masking tape, carefully remove the tape without damaging the wax. You will need these strips again, so hang them from the edge of the work surface.

4 Wet the silk in cold water then immerse it in the turquoise dyebath (see page 25). Gently move the silk around continuously for ten to fifteen minutes to ensure an even penetration of dye. Remove the silk and stir the fix solution into the dyebath. Replace the silk and leave it in the dyebath for forty-five minutes, turning it at regular intervals, then lift it out and gently squeeze out excess dye taking care not to scrunch up the waxed design.

5 Rinse the silk under clean water until the water runs clear, blot the silk with newspaper or paper towels. Hang the scarf on a line, away from direct sunlight, and allow it to dry naturally (preferably in a humid atmosphere) for at least two to three hours. If you hang the scarf indoors, you may want to place some newspaper on the floor to catch the drips.

6 Carefully reposition the strips of masking tape, then feather more wax on the border. This time make longer strokes to take the feathering on to the dyed silk.

7 Remove the backing paper from the leaf masks, then stick each leaf in position.

8 Use the wide brush and wooden stick to spatter wax generously over and around each leaf. Do not overload the brush with wax or you will make large unsightly blobs. Hold the wooden stick over one of the leaf masks then, using short sharp movements, hit the loaded brush against the stick to spatter wax on to the silk around the leaf mask. Repeat the spattering over the other four leaf masks.

9 Carefully remove the leaf masks and masking tape, then use a small round brush to wax long thin lines through the centre line of the borders.

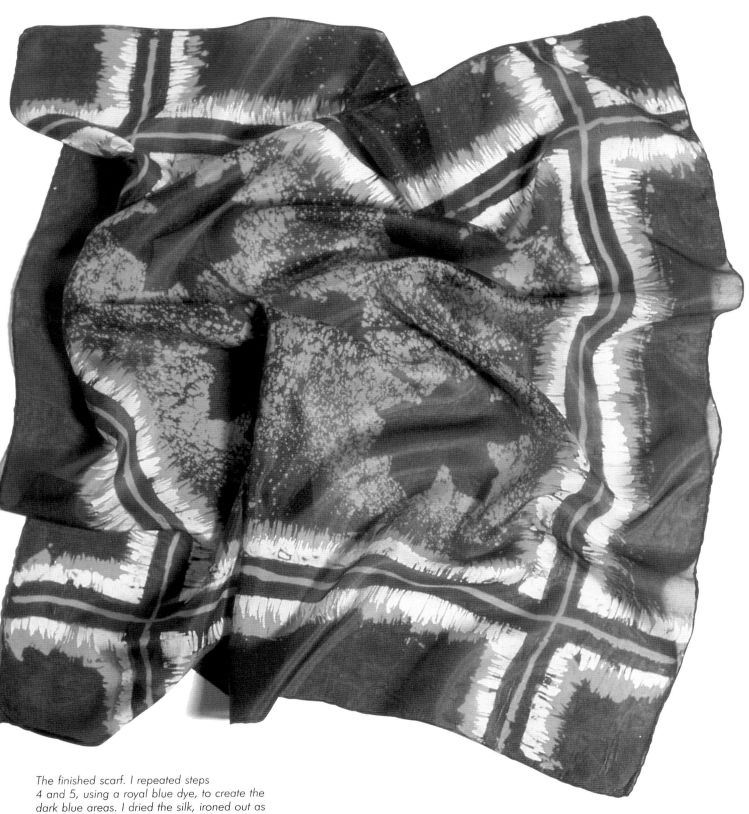

The finished scarf. I repeated steps 4 and 5, using a royal blue dye, to create the dark blue areas. I dried the silk, ironed out as much wax as possible, then dry-cleaned the scarf to remove any residual wax.

Vase of flowers panel

Flowers are a wonderful source of inspiration for batik artists – the diversity of colours, patterns and shapes allows one to interpret them imaginatively. You can treat the batik like a watercolour, applying and blending the dye colours directly on the fabric, wet on wet and wet on dry. You can achieve wonderful effects with a wider range of colours that you cannot obtain when you dip-dye. The dyes spread freely, mixing with each other to form soft or ragged edges depending on whether the fabric is wet or dry. You can also control the flow of colour by waxing outlines of leaves and petals, or by blocking in large areas of the design.

I have chosen a vase of flowers for this project in which I use brushes to apply both the wax and the dye colour. At first you may find it difficult to control your brush strokes, the wax (and dye) may spread and overrun your lines, but do not worry.

YOU WILL NEED

Pretreated cotton fabric (see page 22)

Dye colours: all those listed on page 27 (except black)

Batik wax and wax pot

Soft pencil

Wax brushes

Dye brushes

Paper towel

Frame and pins

Design sketch.

NOTE

Hold a paper towel under the loaded wax brush as you move across the fabric to avoid accidental drips.

If you do spill a blob of unwanted wax, try to incorporate it into your design — maybe it could become part of a flower.

Alternatively, use just the tip of an iron to remove the wax (see page 25), by melting it then blotting it with a paper towel.

1 Use a soft pencil to lightly trace the design on to the fabric, then stretch the fabric on a frame. The pencil lines will gradually disappear as you wax and dye.

2 Dip your brush into the hot wax, then wipe off the excess wax against the side of the pot.

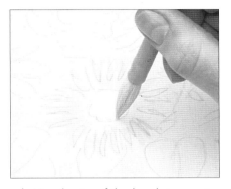

3 Wax those areas of the design you want to keep white. When waxing petals, place the tip of the brush at one end of the petal, gradually press the brush down to increase the width of the stroke, then lift it off.

4 Use the tip of the brush to create tiny highlights.

5 Create squiggles by twisting the brush as you apply pressure.

6 Create random sizes of dots over a controlled area by masking the area with a paper mask, then spattering wax over the exposed area of the fabric.

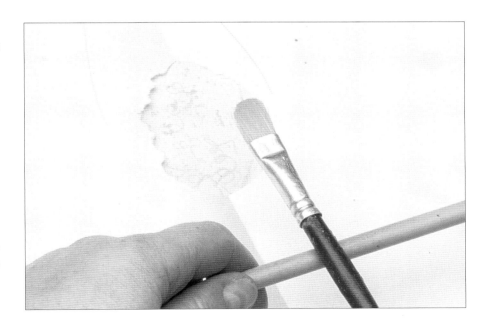

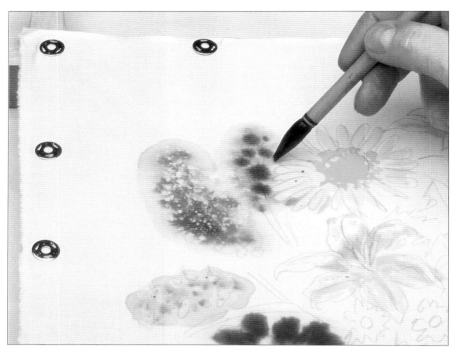

7 Mix a selection of pinks, blues and purples in your palette, diluting the dyes with a little more chemical water to create paler tones. Start colouring the flowers, working some images wet on dry . . .

8 . . . and some wet into wet. Note how the waxed areas resist the dye. When you have finished applying the first set of colours, allow the fabric to dry before adding more wax.

9 Now, work over the design with the wax brush applying wax to the pale tones of the flowers. Your flowers will look more interesting if they feature gradations of colour, so wax over patches of the petals rather than a solid area to allow them to take on different shades of colours.

10 Add more tone to the flowers, then paint the leaves and stems. Do not worry if the dye spreads beyond the pencil lines as this can be corrected later. Leave to dry.

11 Wax over the leaves and stems. Now you can control the line width and decide what to keep as a pale colour. Notice that the waxed dyed areas look darker than the unwaxed areas, and this can be confusing. However, holding the batik up to the light will show the true underlying colours. You can also judge if you have missed any area.

12 Selectively apply more colour to accentuate darker tones and shadowed areas.

NOTE

Sometimes, spots of dye that dry on the wax can seep through to the fabric and cause stains. Such accidents can add texture to, say, one of the flowers in this design. However, if you do not want this to happen, use a paper towel to dab off all the wet dye from the waxed areas of the fabric.

13 Use turquoise and touches of scarlet to colour the vase, wet on wet, blending the colours together on the fabric. Leave to dry, then wax a few horizontal strokes randomly over the foreground area, and wax the zig-zag pattern on the vase. Complete the foreground with a turquoise wash.

14 Check both sides of the fabric to ensure that all flower heads, stems and leaves are fully waxed. Add more wax as necessary. You are now ready to paint the background. Start by using chemical water to dampen the fabric, working down to the top of the table. Do not worry about any colour runs that occur.

15 Apply a royal blue wash over the background, taking it down to the top of the table. All the flowers have been waxed, so you can work long brush strokes right across the fabric.

16 Add touches of this dark colour to the vase and the foreground. Leave the finished painting to dry and fix on the frame overnight. Remove the fabric from the frame, iron out as much wax as possible then dry-clean it to remove any residual wax.

NOTE

The usual rule is not to wax on wet fabric. However I often break this rule to create soft edges. If you apply wax to a slightly damp fabric, not all the wax will penetrate right through, and the applied dyes will creep under the edges of the waxed area to give a blurred effect.

The finished project. Subjects such as this can be stuck on to acid-free, self-adhesive card, then mounted and framed, or stretched round a wooden frame and stapled on the back.

ETCHING & CRACKING

Etching (also referred to as sgraffito) can be used to add controlled shapes and random texture to a batik design. Wax is brushed all over the fabric, then a pointed tool is used to scratch or scrape designs into the wax. When dye is applied, it penetrates through the etched marks into the fabric.

The scratching or etching tools should have a good point that is not too sharp – tapestry needles, the tips of scissor blades, meat skewers and opened-out paperclips can all be used as etching tools.

Another interesting effect is cracking (or marbling), which involves crumpling up an area of waxed fabric to create random cracks, then applying colour. This effect is often regarded as a basic characteristic of batik, but traditionally, cracks in the wax were a sign of poor workmanship. However, the technique can be used to great effect, and the resultant marbled veins can help to unify a picture.

You can create different cracking effects by varying the mixture of wax (see page 22). However, simple control can be achieved by varying the thickness of wax applied to the fabric. Cracks in a thick layer of wax will give strong lines of colour without bleed. On the other hand, cracks applied to a thin layer of wax will allow more colour to penetrate beyond each crack and give a pale colour to the cloth.

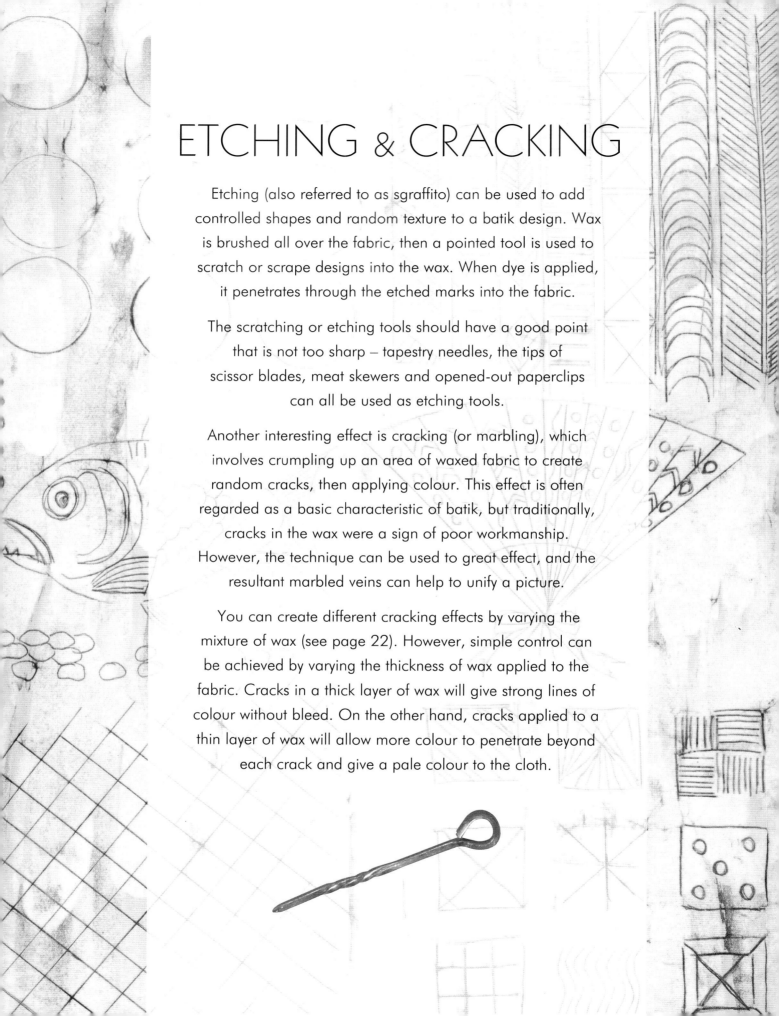

Sgraffito fish panel

I have included this simple project to demonstrate sgraffito and cracking techniques, and the different effects that can be achieved. Although this design is based entirely on sgraffito images, I generally use these techniques just to create detail in my pictures. For example, you can etch twigs, flower stamens, bird feathers, roof tiles or words on signs.

1 Use a pencil or water-soluble pen to transfer the design on to the fabric.

NOTE

You can use batik wax for this project, but you might like to try other blends. If you want to reduce the cracking effect, use a blend that has a high proportion of soft wax. If you want to emphasize the cracks, use a blend high in hard paraffin wax.

If you want crisp clean cracks, put the waxed fabric in a refrigerator for a few minutes. Cold wax is brittle and cracks easily.

NOTE

When applying wax to a large area of fabric on a flat work surface, you must continuously lift the waxed part of the fabric to stop it sticking to the work surface.

If it does become stuck, take care not to crack the wax when you peel it off. You could stretch the fabric on a frame for the waxing stage, but you will have to remove it to a hard surface for the etching stage.

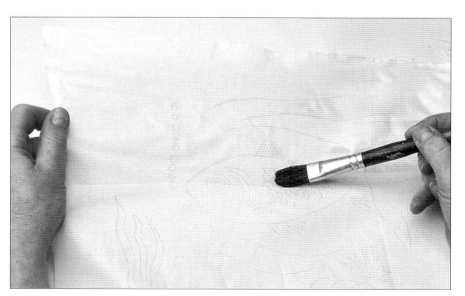

2 Place the fabric on a hard, covered work surface, then use a flat brush to apply a layer of wax over the whole material. Lift the edge of the fabric as you apply the wax. This will help the wax penetrate and harden, and prevent it from adhering to the work surface, as it goes through the fabric.

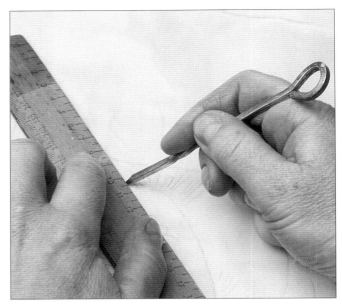

3 Use a meat skewer (or a similar tool) to scratch the outlines of the fish and its scales into the wax. Work slowly and carefully so that you do not pierce or tear the fabric. As you complete each section, turn the fabric over and etch the design from the other side.

4 Use a ruler and the meat skewer to scratch straight lines for the tail and fin. Again, turn the fabric over and scratch through the wax on the back.

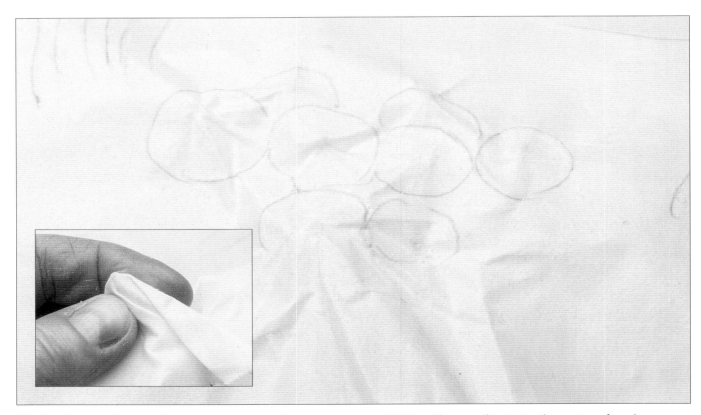

5 Use the tip of a pencil to create texture on the sea anemones. Position the pencil point in the centre of each anemone and crease or scrunch the waxed fabric to create tiny cracks radiating out from the point.

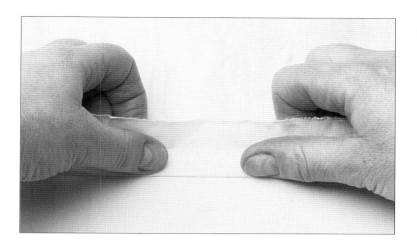

6 Fold one side of the fabric in on itself and crease the fold to form a straight line. Turn the fabric over and remake the fold to break right through the wax. Work another straight line parallel to the first to create a border approximately 12mm (½in) wide. Complete the border by working folds on the other three sides of the fabric.

7 Mix your chosen dye colours, then use a sponge or bristle dye brush to work colour over the etched design. The scratched/creased lines in the wax will allow the exposed fabric to take up the colours, and suddenly the design will become more visible. Work different colours into the fish, reeds, bubbles and starfish, blending them together as you choose.

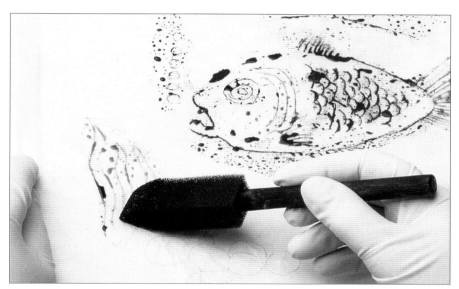

8 Use paper towels to dab off excess dye. Keep changing the towel to stop the transfer of colour from one part of the design to another.

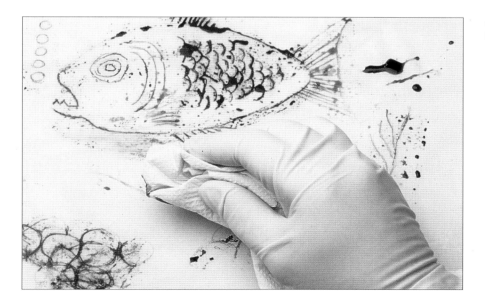

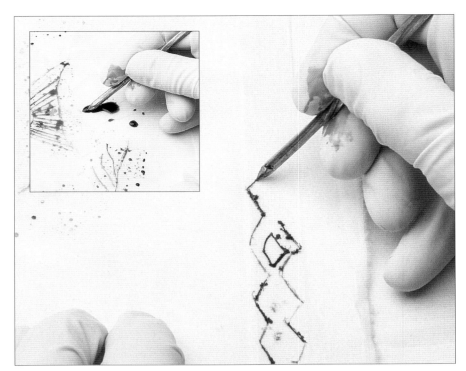

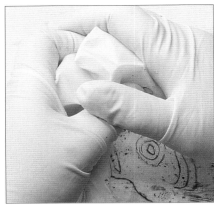

10 A good way of adding texture is to create random cracks in the wax by gently crumpling the fabric between your fingers. For this design, crack parts of the background (corner by corner). Try not to crumple the fabric too much – it is very easy to overdo the effect.

9 You can also etch and 'paint' simultaneously to create controlled shapes. Dip the tip of the meat skewer into some dye then scratch a design through the wax. For this project, I worked a short design within the folded border.

11 Use a stiff dye brush to push colour into the cracked corner areas. Dab off the excess dye with a paper towel, then repeat steps 10–11 in the other three corners.

The finished sgraffito prior to having the wax removed.

The finished sgraffito after having the wax ironed out between newsprint and being dry-cleaned.

You can also get a very effective sgraffito by dyeing the fabric with a range of colours before applying the layer of wax. Then, when you have etched all of the design, dip the whole piece of fabric in a dark coloured dyebath.

Here, I sponged the multicoloured background. When the fabric was dry, I drew the outline of the bird, applied a layer of wax all over the background and waxed the bird's features with a canting (see pages 62–75). I then used a ruler and an etching tool to scribe diagonal lines into the waxed background. Finally, I dip-dyed the fabric in black dye.

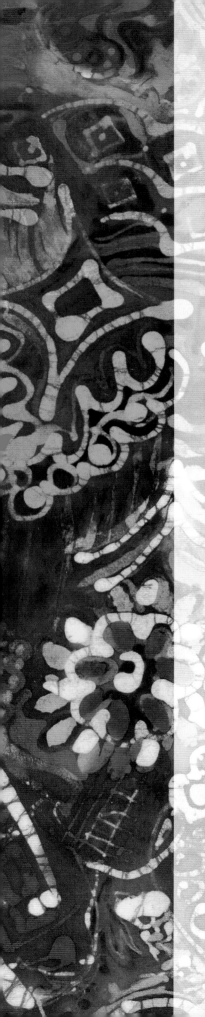

USING CANTINGS

The drawing tool most associated with batik is the canting (tjanting). It is an essential part of batik work in Java, and is used like a pen for drawing lines, for detailing, and for outlining areas prior to filling them in with a brush.

Handling the canting is a matter of some skill. With a little practice and control you will soon be able to draw regular, rhythmic lines of wax whilst barely touching the cloth with the tip of the spout. The best way to get used to handling a canting is to 'doodle'. To begin with you will probably make blobs and accidentally spill the wax from the reservoir. However, you will soon be able to control the flow of wax and draw lines fluently. The regular filling of the canting will very soon become an automatic movement.

I have included two projects in this section: a doodled lampshade, where the canting is used to create an abstract design; and a picture of a bowl of fruit, where the canting is used in much the same way as a gutta pen in silk painting, to outline different areas of the composition. These wax lines act as barriers to contain the dye colour within each enclosed area.

Doodled lampshade

Batik colours look particularly brilliant when the fabric is lit from behind. An easy way to show off this brilliance is to hang a batik in a window, but care must be taken to ensure that sunlight does not fade the colours over the months. Fibre-reactive dyes are particularly resistant to light. However, some colours may fade, so it is better to choose a north facing window.

Another way of displaying the batik is to light it from behind with a spotlight. Alternatively you could batik a lampshade, and I have chosen this as the project to introduce doodling with a canting. It is quite easy to cover a lampshade. You simply wax and dye a design on paper or fabric and then stick or sew the finished batik on to the lampshade.

As usual, do experiment with the canting by taking the wax for a walk! Dot, doodle, or draw with the wax. Have fun!

1 Use the lampshade and a large sheet of paper to make a pattern. Practise rolling the shade on your paper to ensure you can get the complete shape within the space available. Draw the outline by following its course with a pencil close to the wire. Mark the start and the end of the circumference, and add a small overlap.

2 Cut out the paper pattern and wrap it around the lampshade to check it fits. Pin the pattern to the fabric and cut to size.

3 Dampen the fabric with water and spread it out on newsprint. There are no white areas in the design, so apply random diagonal stripes of scarlet and golden yellow dye. Use touches of lemon yellow dye to blend the colours together. Leave to dry naturally. Before waxing renew the paper on the work surface.

4 Place the canting in the hot wax to warm up for a few minutes.

5 Half-fill the canting reservoir with wax, then lift it out of the pot. Hot wax will flow too freely at first, so allow it to drip over the pot for a second or two, then. . .

6 . . . place a paper towel under the reservoir and spout as you transfer the canting to the fabric.

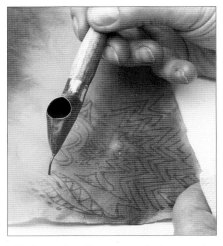

7 Start doodling your design on the fabric, wiping the nozzle on the towel at the end of each stroke. Hold the canting slightly at an angle and 'float' the spout across the surface. Do not press it on the fabric as this will prevent the flow of wax. Do not worry if you accidentally drip wax on to the fabric, just incorporate it as part of your design. If you camouflage it well enough, it will look as if it was intentional.

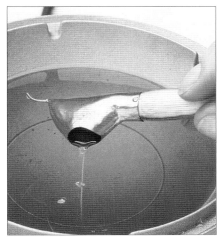

8 As the flow from the spout slows down (this will be due to the canting getting cool), empty the reservoir into the wax pot and recharge it with hot wax. The procedure of regularly filling the reservoir and placing the paper towel under the spout at the end of each stroke will soon become rhythmical and second nature.

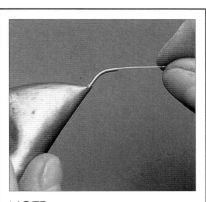

NOTE

Occasionally the canting can become blocked if specks of dirt, bits of paper towel or thread from the fabric fall into the wax. In such a case fine fuse wire can be gently pushed through the spout.

If you leave the canting to cool on a hard surface, you may damage the spout when you try to pick it up. Prop the handle on a piece of wood so that the reservoir is not in contact with the work surface.

9 When you have finished waxing the design right across the fabric, use mahogany and cerise dyes to add more stripes of colour. Use chemical water to soften the edges. The waxed design should come to life as these darker colours are added. Use a paper towel to dab off excess dye, then leave the fabric to fix and dry (see page 42).

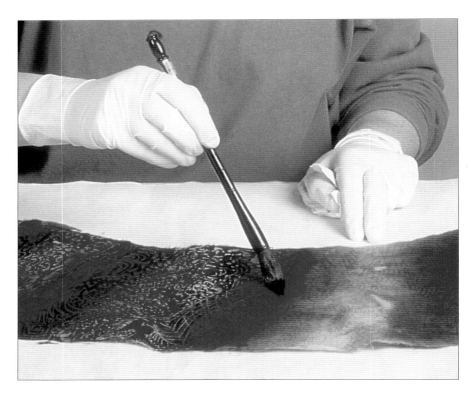

10 Iron out the wax between sheets of newsprint and dry-clean if necessary. Finally, apply a coat of spray adhesive to the back of the fabric and secure it round the lampshade. Overlap the edges and make sure they are stuck down. If you have any braid, put it round the top and bottom of the shade to give it a more finished look.

The finished lampshade.

Bowl of fruit panel

Fruits have very simple, easily identifiable shapes which can be drawn with a canting. Wax round the outline of each fruit, and then colour and blend subtle tones within the enclosed areas. If you do not want pure white lines, then dye the fabric in a very pale wash of yellow or pink dye before your first waxing. Also choose a small spouted canting as the picture can be spoiled by thick waxed outlines.

To counter the structured shape of the fruit, I decided to use salt to add texture to the background. Salt produces beautiful random patterns and textures when it is sprinkled on to fabric while the dye is still damp. As the fabric dries, the salt absorbs the moisture and 'pulls' the dyes into fantastic patterns.

Different types of salt produce different effects, so experiment beforehand on a sample piece of fabric. Try fine cooking salt, table salt, coarse rock salt and dishwasher salt to see how fascinating and unpredictable the results can be. It all depends on the dampness of the fabric; the tension at which it is stretched; how concentrated the dyes are; and how long the salt is left on for. Try to sprinkle the salt evenly over the fabric, as too much in some areas can spoil the overall patterned effect.

YOU WILL NEED
Pretreated white cotton (see page 22)
Water-soluble marker pen
Frame and pins
Wax and wax pot
Canting
Dye colours: all colours listed on page 27
Dye brushes
Salt for texture

Design sketch.

1 Use a water-soluble marker pen or soft pencil to trace the design on to the fabric.

2 Stretch the fabric on a frame then, using a kystka or small-spouted canting, wax over all the solid lines of the design (the dotted lines show where colours should be blended at a later stage). Check the back of the fabric to ensure that all waxed lines penetrate right through the fabric and that there are no gaps in the outline. Remember that dyes can bleed through the tiniest of gaps and spoil the design. Fill in any areas, such as the highlights on the grapes, that you want to be white.

3 Start applying pale base colours to the fruit with quick controlled strokes. Work wet on wet or wet on dry, depending on how intense a colour you want. The dye spreads into the surrounding fibres and stops when it reaches the wax line. Do not worry if some dye spreads through tiny gaps in the waxed outline.

4 Slow the spread of colour by drying the fabric with a hairdryer, repair the broken outline with a touch of wax, then work the adjacent fruits. The new colours will mask the previous 'error'.

5 When you have finished applying base colours to the fruit and the bowl, allow the fabric to dry. Then, wax the lighter areas and apply darker shades of dye to create shape and form, and to develop the areas in shadow.

6 Apply wax to any previously unwaxed parts of the design – all the individual fruits and the bowl must be completely covered with wax. Turn the frame upside down and check the underside of the fabric to ensure complete wax penetration. Brush wax over any bare areas.

7 Turn the fabric right side up, then use a large sponge brush and chemical water to dampen all the fabric.

8 Use the sponge brush and a pale turquoise dye to lay a wash across the top of the design. Dilute the colour as you work down the picture.

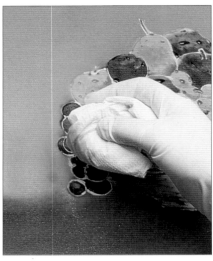

11 Use a small spray bottle to spatter cerise dye randomly over the still-wet turquoise background.

9 Wash royal blue across the bottom of the design. Blend the edge where it meets the turquoise with a touch of water.

10 Use a paper towel to soak up any puddles of dye that form on the surface of the fabric.

NOTE
Wear a filter-pad face mask when using a spray bottle to avoid inhaling airborne dye mist.

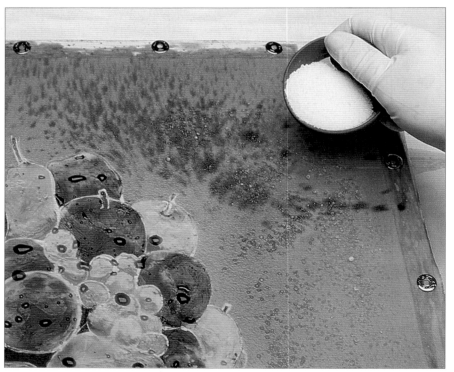

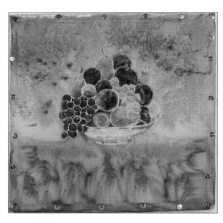

The finished picture, prior to having the wax removed.

12 Sprinkle salt over the wet dye colours and watch as the salt starts to produce a random texture. Leave to dry naturally. Alternatively, when you are happy with the result, use a hairdryer to stop the action. However, take care not to blow any wet salt crystals across the fabric as the absorbed dye could make marks on other parts of the fabric. When the fabric is completely dry, brush off the salt crystals, then remove the wax (see page 25).

Opposite
The finished picture, after all the wax has been removed. You may notice that the outlines round some of the grapes vary in thickness. This is caused by wax flooding out of the canting at the beginning of each stroke. If you do not want this to happen, start the stroke on a paper towel and run the canting on to the fabric.

Boat with reflections panel

Batik lends itself to creating water effects, especially reflections, so I have chosen a simple watery subject for this project, in which I use brushes and cantings to apply the wax. Brushes are good for blocking out large areas of fabric and for some of the larger ripples, whereas the tiny spout of a canting is ideal for waxing details on the boat and for the finer ripples.

In this picture I want a red boat on blue water, but I do not want a white outline around the boat or its reflection. To achieve this effect you must boil out the wax half way through the project. Start by enclosing the outlines of the areas you want to colour red with wax, then apply the cerise dye. Next, boil out the wax, cover the red areas with fresh wax, then apply the blue dyes.

YOU WILL NEED

Cotton fabric

Water-soluble pen or soft pencil

Frame and pins

Batik wax and wax pot

Cantings and wax brushes

Fixed dye colours: cerise, royal blue, navy blue

Dye brushes

Paper towel

An old saucepan

Washing soda

Tongs or old wooden spoon

Design sketch.

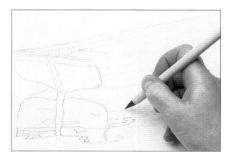

1 Use a water-soluble marker pen or a soft pencil to trace the design on to the fabric, then stretch the fabric on a frame.

2 Use a small wax brush to wax round the outline of the boat, the small buoy and their reflections. These outlines are to contain the cerise dye used to paint the boat and buoy, and to prevent this colour spreading over the water. This wax will be boiled out before colouring the water.

3 Use a brush to wax the top front edge of the boat, then use the small canting or kystka to wax highlights on the seats and the bow of the boat. Add a small highlight on the buoy, then wax ripples (that are to remain white) in the boat's reflection.

4 Use a small brush and cerise dye to paint inside the waxed outlines of the boat, the buoy and their reflections. The dye will spread out to the waxed line and no further. Leave the dye to fix properly by allowing the fabric to dry for at least twelve hours (preferably in a moist atmosphere).

5 Now remove the wax. Boil up a saucepan of water, add one teaspoon of washing soda, then immerse the fabric in the water and boil it for five minutes. Use a wooden spoon to lift the fabric out of the saucepan, then plunge the fabric into a bowl of cold water. The wax solidifies on the surface of the fabric so that it can be rubbed or scraped off. Repeat the boiling process until all the wax has been removed. Allow the water to get cold and remove *all* traces of wax before disposing of the water. Even though you have removed all the wax, never pour wax water down a drain. Wash the batik in soapy water, dry and iron out the creases.

6 Use the water-soluble pen to re-draw the outline of the boat, then re-stretch the fabric on a frame.

7 Wax over the areas of the boat, the buoy and their reflections that you want to keep red and white. Leave tiny gaps between each plank of the boat – subsequent dyes will darken these and help define the shape of the boat. Leave some of the red areas unwaxed so that, when you paint the next dye (a blue) over it, a shadow will be created.

8 Use the canting to wax ripples in the water.

9 Paint a royal blue dye over all of the fabric, then leave to dry.

10 Use a brush and a canting to wax more ripples in the water and reflections. Vary the shape and thickness of these marks, and remember that they will be the paler blue in the finished picture.

11 Now brush the navy blue dye over the fabric. Leave to dry, then hold the picture up against a light to see the effect. If necessary, add more waxed ripples then apply more blue dye to create even darker areas of water.

12 Define the shape and form of the boat by paying particular attention to the shadows and reflections in areas of water. If you want to emphasise these, wax the water and the boat, then apply more navy blue dye.

The finished picture before (right) and after (below) having the wax removed (see page 25).

I have used a simple design for this project. More complicated designs can have many more stages of waxing, dyeing and boiling. Remember the principal of working from the lightest to darkest tones, and keep holding the fabric up to the light to check your progress and see how the picture comes to life.

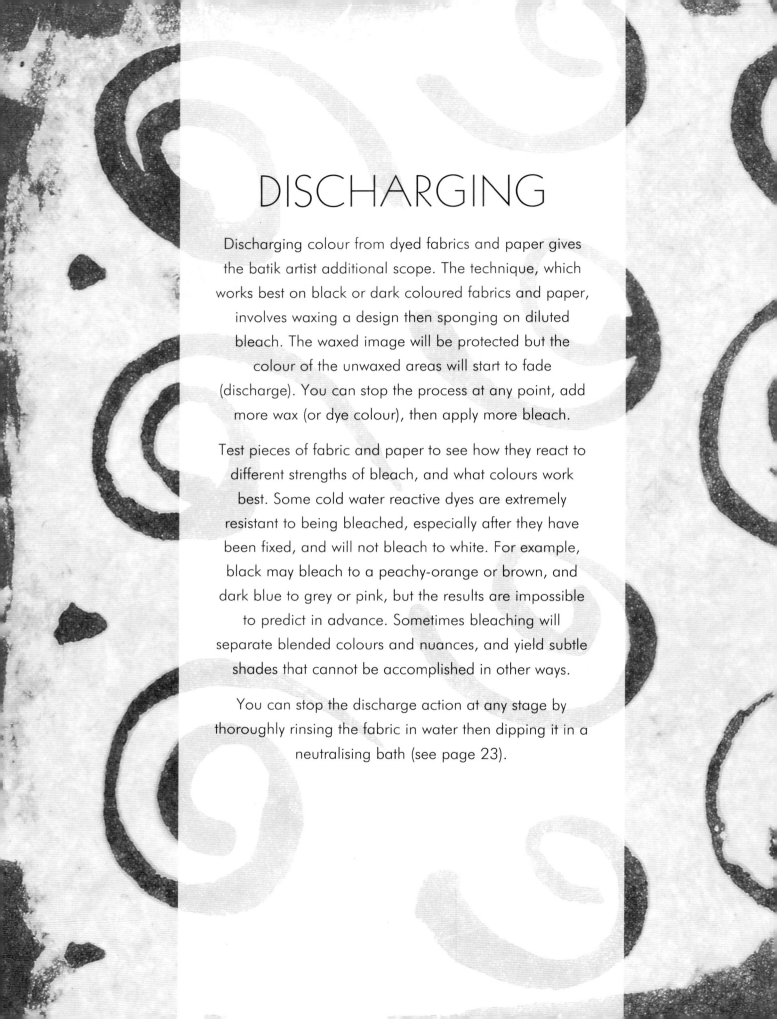

DISCHARGING

Discharging colour from dyed fabrics and paper gives the batik artist additional scope. The technique, which works best on black or dark coloured fabrics and paper, involves waxing a design then sponging on diluted bleach. The waxed image will be protected but the colour of the unwaxed areas will start to fade (discharge). You can stop the process at any point, add more wax (or dye colour), then apply more bleach.

Test pieces of fabric and paper to see how they react to different strengths of bleach, and what colours work best. Some cold water reactive dyes are extremely resistant to being bleached, especially after they have been fixed, and will not bleach to white. For example, black may bleach to a peachy-orange or brown, and dark blue to grey or pink, but the results are impossible to predict in advance. Sometimes bleaching will separate blended colours and nuances, and yield subtle shades that cannot be accomplished in other ways.

You can stop the discharge action at any stage by thoroughly rinsing the fabric in water then dipping it in a neutralising bath (see page 23).

Apple panel

In this project I discharge an apple design on a piece of commercially-dyed black fabric. If you cannot find a suitable fabric for discharging, you can pre-dye the fabric in a dark colour, rinse, dry, then discharge the dye colour. There is no such thing as a 'pure' black dye, and I make my own black by combining three colours (red, yellow and navy blue). Alternatively, a deep black can be mixed using one part navy blue with three parts black dye.

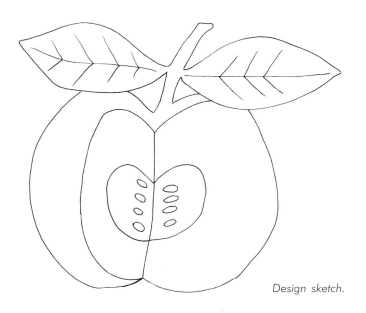

Design sketch.

SAFETY NOTES

Bleach is a strong oxidising agent and very corrosive. Follow the manufacturer's instructions for use and disposal.

Avoid inhaling bleach fumes.

NOTE

As a rule, the stronger the bleach solution, the faster the reaction. However, fast discharges often result in stark contrasts of colour.

Cheap household bleach can be used straight from the container, but stronger, thicker solutions should be diluted. For a fast reaction use one part bleach with one part water. For a slower, more controlled reaction, dilute one part bleach with up to five parts of water.

Bleach weakens the fibres of the fabric, so take care not to leave the fabric in the solution too long — never more than 5 minutes. Time the discharge carefully, and note the times taken to achieve different shades of colour.

Never use bleach on silk or wool, it destroys the fibres and the fabric disintegrates.

Bleach mixtures can be saved and reused.

Bleach tends to break down the wax and make it less adhesive. If you are going to disharge at different stages, you may have to rewax some areas.

1 Use dressmakers' carbon paper and a pencil to transfer the design onto the fabric.

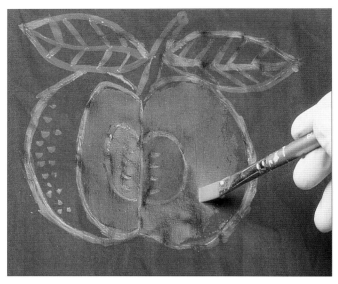

2 Use a small brush to wax all the traced outlines that are to remain black. Check on the back of the fabric to ensure that the wax has penetrated right through. If not, rewax the design on the back.

3 Wearing rubber gloves, dilute the bleach with a little water in a jar, then use a nylon brush (not a bristle one as the bleach will destroy it) to brush the bleach over the whole image. The colour will begin to discharge.

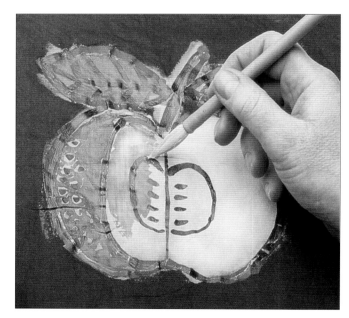

4 As the colour starts to fade, selectively add more bleach to the areas you want to be the lightest. Here, I want to make the right-hand cut segment the lightest, the left-hand one slightly darker, and the apple skin and leaves even darker. When the outer skin colour is a mid grey, stop the discharge action of the bleach by thoroughly rinsing the fabric in clean water, then dipping it in the neutralising bath for ten minutes. Rinse again to remove all traces of the neutraliser, then leave to dry.

5 Brush wax over the areas you want to keep darker – the outer skin, the left-hand cut segment and the leaves. Leave gaps round the spots on the skin so they can bleach lighter.

Opposite
The finished panel.

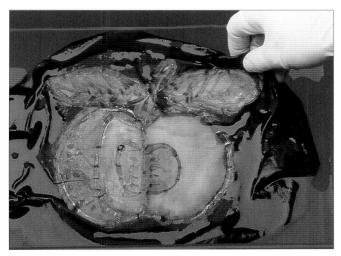

6 Arrange the fabric in a shallow tray so that the apple design is flat but the corners are scrunched up slightly. Pour in some diluted bleach. This time I want a textured background so I am not worried if the whole fabric is not fully in contact with the bleach.

7 Watch the background colours start to fade. Sometimes, the bleach creates dark edges which can be used to advantage in a design. When the right-hand cut segment is as bright as you want it to be, stop the discharge again. Rinse and neutralise the fabric again, then rinse in mild detergent and leave to dry. Finally, iron out the wax (see page 25).

Gallery

Rooftops

On a recent visit to southwest China, I happened to spend a night in a Miao village during a local festival. At 3.30 in the morning, I was woken by the noise of a fire cracker that had been set off under my bedroom window and got up to investigate. The view from my window was breathtaking. A mist was rising from the rooftops and mingling with the smoke from the fire cracker.

In this painting of the scene I started with a grey, Japanese silk paper. I waxed the lines for roof tiles, painted over them with a brown dye, then applied green dye to the trees. I discharged areas of the sky and some highlights on the buildings. Notice that the paper discharges to a pale pink colour. The silk threads in the paper help give the impression of mist. For this particular subject I did not remove the wax, having decided that it added just the right type of texture to the rooftops.

Walking home

This batik was waxed and dip-dyed, starting with pale rose pink, then gradually adding more wax and dipping in a succession of darker dyebaths. I used a meat skewer and the etching technique (see page 56) to create the spokes of the wheel, before dipping the fabric in the final dyebath.

McCurdy Wharf

Every summer I visit Nova Scotia, Canada, and I find that part of the world a wonderful source of subject matter. Water and reflections are always a challenge, but batik is the perfect medium for portraying them. For this batik I used cantings and a brush to apply the wax. As usual I started by waxing the white areas, then gradually applied a multitude of shades of pale colours, waxing and overlaying each colour to build up the darkest tones. I also used the discharge technique selectively to create texture.

Leaping salmon

Batik is a perfect technique for depicting splashes of water. You can flick and spatter wax, apply the dyes, then spatter again. This batik, created by Anya Keith, an eighteen-year-old student of mine, has a wonderful sense of movement – the salmon really does look as if it is leaping out of the water.

Opposite
Fishing for crabs
Water and rocks are always attractive subjects for batik. This one features Sally, the daughter of a friend of mine, searching for hermit crabs. I used a number of different tools and combined many batik effects to achieve this result.

Stamped flowers

You can make wonderful flower designs from the most unlikely shapes. This design was waxed with lots of different pastry cutters, with just a little brushed wax to fill in the background. A heart-shaped pastry cutter is particularly good for petals. You can also overlap them to create different patterns.

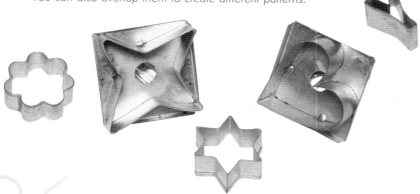

Opposite
Brushed floral scarf

The waxed areas on this scarf were applied with a brush. I started the batik by painting an assortment of colours freely on the silk. I waxed areas to retain the pinks and greens, then overlaid more colours. I continued waxing and dyeing, building up the colours from the lightest to the darkest. Finally, when all the areas I wanted to keep had been waxed, I dip-dyed the whole scarf in the final colour.

Not out!

Cricket has been one of my sources of inspiration for many years. I love to capture the movement of cricketers in action as well as recreating the highlights and tones of grey in their clothing. I will only batik cricketers in their Test Match whites.

Opposite

Don in his greenhouse

Greenhouses and conservatories are also included in my list of favourite subjects. The way that light filters through the glass and casts shadows on plants and stones is something I enjoy trying to capture. In this batik, I waxed and dyed the colours until I had completed all the detail. The last stage was to lay a dark wash over the whole picture, and suddenly Don came to life!

Scottish burn

Batik is an ideal painting medium for depicting trees and leaves, and I could not resist painting this burn which is close to where I used to live in Scotland. Using the tip of a round brush and the technique called pointillism I waxed and dyed the dappled effect of the leaves and water.

Spring and bluebells

This bluebell glade is in a wood just down the road from my home. In spring, the leaf colours are fresh and bright, and the bluebells range from pale blue to purple. As usual, I waxed and dyed colours from the palest to the the darkest. I waxed with a brush and a canting, and I used a scrunched-up paper towel to wax the bluebells and most of the leaves. I used a brush to apply all the pale colours then, having protected them with wax, I turned to dip-dyeing for the dark shades.

Opposite

Venetian canal

Venice has always been a favourite source of inspiration for artists in all media. In this batik, I particularly enjoyed the challenge of reproducing the reflections in the canal, and the waxing and overlaying of pastel colours to create the soft-coloured, flaking walls of the buildings.

Venetian reflection

This wax resist picture shows just how versatile batik can be. Here, rather than working on cotton, I collaged layers of tissue paper by waxing, dyeing and discharging the design. I used the tip of the iron to melt some waxed areas to allow the colours of the lower layers of tissue to shine through. It took some time to complete, but the resultant three-dimensional effect is very difficult to achieve on fabric.

A lemon and a half

This batik and the one below are part of a set of different fruits, in which I tried to recreate some old botanical paintings that were fashionable a few centuries ago. I built up the colours by dip-dyeing, using the cracking technique in the background. I waxed the areas I wanted to keep white, then dipped the fabric in a pale yellow dye. I then waxed the background right up to the outline of the fruit and their leaves, then concentrated on waxing and dyeing them. Finally, I fully waxed the fruit and the leaves, carefully crumpled the background, then dipped the whole fabric in a mid-brown dye. There is only subtle cracking, as I wanted to create a mottled effect similar to that of old parchment.

An apple and a half

Opposite

Church walk

I love to try and capture the contrast between bright highlights and deep shadows, but it can be quite difficult to decide when to stop applying layers of dye, especially when most of the fabric is covered with wax. When I had removed all the wax from this batik, I found that the foreground was not dark enough, so I rewaxed the sunlit area and painted a weak grey-blue wash all over.

Index